Christians On Assignment
Talking About Obedience

Paulette Denise

Christians On Assignment 2010, revised in 2024 ©

Scripture quotations are from:

Scripture quotations marked (AMP) are taken from the Amplified Bible, Old Testament, copyright © 1965, 1987 by the Zondervan Corporation. The Amplified Bible, New Testament, copyright © 1954, 1958, 1962, 1964, 1965, 1987 by the Lockman Foundation.

All Rights Reserved. No part of this publication may be reproduced or transmitted in any form or by any means, electronic or mechanical, including photocopy, recording, or any information storage and retrieval system, except for brief quotations in reviews, without the written permission of the author.

Printed in the United States of America

ISBN 978-0-9831341-0-7

Copyright © 2024 by Paulette Denise

A Portion Ministries

DEDICATION

I would like to dedicate this entire project to the Lord Jesus Christ, the Savior of my life, and the world. To all of my family, friends, and associates that have been a part of my life and given any input on this project – entirely too many to name, just know I appreciate each and every one of you. To the entire generation of *Obedient Christian's on Assignment.*

~Paulette Denise~

On Assignment

Christians On Assignment – Talking About Obedience
Table of Contents

INTRODUCTION		**9**
0.1	Purpose of the book	11
0.2	Looking at obedience	12
0.3	Obedience and faith	16
CHAPTER 1 – JESUS FAITH		**18**
1.1	Defining faith	18
1.2	Faith and beliefs	19
1.3	Faith and doubt	20
1.4	Faith and authority	22
1.5	The triune God	26
CHAPTER 2 – ON ASSIGNMENT		**29**
2.1	How do I know?	29
2.2	Self evaluations	29
2.3	Work out your salvation	34
2.4 & 2.5	Intimacy with God	35
2.6	Hunger and thirst for God	37
2.7	Desire…	39
2.8	What type of vessel are you?	41

2.9	On Assignment— Training/Preparation	50
2.10	Timing and Details	53
2.11	I Won't Complain	56
2.12	Humble and Content	58
2.13	Patience Train…	61

CHAPTER 3 – FAILURE TO APPEAR — **65**

3.1	Resurrection Power	65
3.2	Questioning?	66
3.3	Mentoring – Divine connections	70

CHAPTER 4 – DEALING WITH THE HEART — **75**

4.1	Open before God	75
4.2	A clean heart	76
4.3	Defining heart	78
4.4	Jesus and your heart	81
4.5	Holiness – the worshipper's heart	84
4.6	In spirit and truth	86
4.7	Guard your heart	87
4.8	Heart confession	89

CHAPTER 5 – NOT OF THIS WORLD — **91**

5.1	The world hates you	91
5.2	Strangers and aliens	92
5.3	Do You Really KNOW Him?	93
5.4	Get the "L" out	96

CHAPTER 6 – THE GREAT FALL — **98**

6.1	Temptation	98
6.2	Get back up, run back in	100
6.3	Talking About ALL Things…	106
6.4	Better or bitter?	107

CHAPTER 7 – DISTRACTIONS — 110

7.1	Detours	110
7.2	Thorns	112
7.3	Speed-bump or brick-wall?	117
7.4	Busy distractions	117

CHAPTER 8 – PRAYER & FASTING — 122

8.1	Warrior	122
8.2	Dressed For Battle	123
8.3	Fasting	128
8.4	A Consecrated Life	132
8.5	Pray, pray, PRAY…	134

CHAPTER 9 – RECONCILING THE HEARTS — 136

9.1	Malachi 4	136
9.2	Our part	137
9.3	Male Man Needed	143
9.4	Flock of Men	145
9.5	Following God	147
9.6	Fatherless	148

CHAPTER 10 - FOR SUCH A TIME AS THIS — 150

CHAPTER 11 – KINGDOM READY — 153

11.1 Kingdom ready 153

11.2 Eternity Minded 153

11.3 The Great Commandment and The Great Commission 155

11.4 Conclusion 157

INTRODUCTION

Preface

While writing this project, I have experienced attack, after attack, after attack. A constant trial! No area of my life has been untouched: my finances, family/children, reputation, character, integrity, sanity, physical body, desire for ministry and helping others – I mean every aspect of my life has been attacked and tried. I have wanted to give up on this project numerous times – not just the book project, but even life itself. But God! All I can say is that I have had firsthand experience of His strength being made perfect in my weakness – totally relying on the sufficient grace of God. I have truly learned what "the joy of the Lord is my strength" means firsthand. As well, active opportunities to praise instead of panic. I have learned to stick to the script – the written word of God concerning me; as well the daily prescriptions of eating, meditating, and delighting in the word of God. All the glory belongs to God.

2024 Updated Preface

Wow! Fourteen years have passed since the first printing of this project, and the previous preface is a resounding echo and repeat from then to now! Everything that could be shaken has been shaken, and even more. My resolve is more and amplified with passion!

The renewal of the mind journey of Romans 12:2 has empowered me in the various *Assignments* I've encountered since the first edition. The Passion Translation of Romans 12:2 reads: *Stop imitating the ideals and opinions of the culture around you, but be inwardly transformed by the Holy Spirit through a total reformation of how you think. This will empower you to discern God's will as you live a beautiful life, satisfying and perfect in his eyes.*

Introduction – A Portion Volume Two

0.1 *Purpose of the book*
A Portion Volume Two – Christians On Assignment – *Obedience*.

I had just completed A Portion Volume One in March 2002, when I received the subject of Volume Two. However, I did not begin writing or gathering materials for almost another seven years. I had to finish walking out several *assignments* and see all the good possibilities of *assignments* that I could have chosen to discuss, such as: owning a business, singing, writing, teaching, preaching, mentoring and so on that I really had to go before the Lord seeking the exact focus of this book. Since all Christians have a common *assignment* to be witnesses for the Lord Jesus Christ, I wanted to talk about something universal and critical to successfully fulfilling any Christian *assignment*. Notice I said <u>fulfilling;</u> there may be various sub- or mini- *assignments* along the way to fulfilling your main *assignment*, but the common denominator of all the *assignments* you will face in your Christian walk is OBEDIENCE.

A Portion Volume Two – Christians On Assignment – Talking About Obedience is not meant to be a "how-to" book, but rather a tool that can be used during your preparation process. As you read through this book, store-up the information you come across and allow the Holy Spirit to bring back to mind the nuggets you learn as you move forward in your walk. The purpose of this book is to act as a guide, making you aware of potential obstacles that you may encounter in your Christian walk and providing tools to help you navigate around them. I expect you to do as I do when reading material based on the bible: "eat the meat and leave the bones". That is to say, there may be some topics addressed that do not apply to you (at least not right now), so leave that *portion* on the side of the plate; it may become "meat" for you in another season.

Personally, I like to study in the amplified bible because it expounds on the Hebrew and Greek meanings of words, all the scripture references I use are from the amplified bible unless otherwise stated. This project contains a heavy amount of scripture references and different topics describing the process I went through personally to achieve understanding of the texts and how each relates to *obedience*. Additionally, I have included in the table of contents a reference of topics discussed to make it easy for you to navigate back to specific points in the future. With that said, let's get started...

0.2 Looking at obedience
The dictionary defines "obedient" as submissive to the restraint or command of authority; willing to obey. Putting this in context with the goal of this book, obedience means we are willing to obey the authority of God – which is found in His word. This is truly easier said than done because there are several hard sayings in the bible, and difficult to understand passages. Some scriptures actually seem to be irrelevant to us today. Throughout this project, I plan on taking text and helping describe how to be obedient from modern day scenarios and understandings.

> *(Proverbs 31:15) She rises while it is yet night and gets [spiritual] food for her household and assigns her maids their tasks.*

When the Lord led me to this scripture as the theme of my call, I had a few questions. I understood the first *portion*, since I had been getting up early in the morning to pray and study the word of God. I could see how doing this had been preparing spiritual meals for me and my family, as well as for those to whom I was allowed to minister to. But my big question was, who were "her maids" or as in the NIV "her servant girls"? My question to God was "I don't have any of these, so who are You talking about?" His response showed me that my thoughts truly are not His thoughts, and that His thoughts are better than mine. The response was, "Correct, *you* don't have any maids or servant girls, but **I** have many." WOW, what an awesome God!

The God of the universe wanted to deliver a message to His people, and He had chosen me to deliver this *Portion*. I was elated! So I immediately started making notes of all of the things that the Lord allowed my spiritual eyes to see. Those early morning sessions were what I like to call my threshing floor. And as in biblical times when the grain from the harvest was brought to the threshing floor to be stored up, I gathered the things that I had gleaned from various books, sermon messages, and personal studies along with all I had stored up from those early morning sessions, and I began to prepare spiritual food for my household and His servants.

In *A Portion Volume One*, I stated that my simple *obedience* test was regarding oral hygiene. My test was to just add a few extra steps each day to my daily regimen. This may seem like a silly test, but I will back up here and give a little history. I was taught by my mother as well in elementary school to brush my teeth three times a day, or after each meal, and to floss daily. Although, I was taught this, I neglected this teaching and only brushed my teeth once a day – in the morning when I woke up. As a child, I didn't understand why I was told to do this, so not realizing its importance, I did not fully obey. As a consequence of my disobedience to this teaching; I experienced serious dental issues in my early adult life. With all the major dental work I had to have done, I probably made quite a few dentists a considerable amount of income. The bottom line is this: if I had been doing what I had been taught to do at a young age all along, this would not have become such a large problem. Many of you reading this book brush and floss regularly which says to me that you understand the importance of it. So like you were taught to have a daily regimen for taking care of your mouth, you must also train yourself to have a daily regimen for taking care of your spiritual relationship.

I stated in *A Portion Volume One*, that I am still *"in the process"* myself. I ask the Lord daily to assist me in living what He is inspiring me to write. I have known for over 10 years that my simple *obedience* test is my dental hygiene. Yet I am sitting here in a new dental office, and to quote what the dentist just said to me after taking x-rays and examining my teeth, "You don't floss much, do you?" This comment brought me to immediate tears (I'm glad he left the exam room). I was crying because I realized just then, that although I have improved in many other areas, I still had not met God's standard in this *obedience* test. He used an unknowing dentist to give me the progress report.

How many times have you experienced this? Your test may not be oral hygiene like mine but maybe your test is to lose a little weight, yet every time you go to purchase something new, you keep having to get a larger size, instead of a smaller size. Or maybe it is to clean out your closet, but you close the door then tell everyone – "don't open that" as you keep walking by it. Or maybe it is to visit elderly relatives or serve as a volunteer at your church and you keep putting it off until some emergency occurs that forces you to act and then you feel a sense of disappointment in yourself. This can be an awkward space to be in. My advice is to acknowledge your deficiency as soon as you notice it. Change (or *obedience*) begins in your heart; once you make the decision to change, develop a plan for how you will make the changes. Set a timeline and find someone to help you hold yourself accountable to follow through with the appropriate actions.

Obedience can be referred to as a compass or map directing you to the center of God's will. When traveling, it is important to regularly monitor your compass to ensure that you are going in the desired direction. An example of this in my life occurred in July 2002 when I relocated from Oakland California to Tulsa Oklahoma. Although I had traveled to Tulsa by airplane, I had never driven there. I mapped out the route, using three different resources just to be on the safe side, and planned out my trip. As I drove, I continually consulted my map and all along the road I regularly looked for the road signs that showed the direction of "East". Other's lives were affected by my ability to stay on course, since I had my two daughters in the car with me. My family and friends at home were seriously concerned about me taking such a long journey as a single woman with two small children in the car. Yet I knew that this was *my* journey, and that God would protect us. The journey was a success! We made it to Tulsa just as I had scheduled in my mapping out the plans, all the way down to the estimated time of arrival (including various planned stops along the way). In Jeremiah 29:11 God says, *For I know the plans I have for you," declares the LORD, "plans to prosper you and not to harm you, plans to give you hope and a future.* This became a living example of walking out God's plan for my life and it positioned me to experience more of God's plan.

Obedience, my friend, is the same way. You may know your desired destination (to be in the center of God's will); you have your road map (the bible) you may have consulted various sources regarding your trip (the church, bible teachers, the Holy Spirit); but until you get on that first highway, and begin to follow God's plan step-by-step, and allow Him to take you places that you have never been, show you things you have never seen, while regularly consulting your compass (*obedience* to God's word and the leading of the Holy Spirit) along the way, you will never arrive to your desired destination in the center of God's will. God does have a permissive will, meaning that He will permit you to make decisions based on your own free will – oh but to be in the center of God's will by saying yes to His plans/leading/guiding!

0.3 Obedience and faith
Obedience to the word of God is what caused my faith in the power of the word of God to grow.

> (Joshua 1:8) This Book of the Law shall not depart out of your mouth, but you shall meditate on it day and night, that you may **observe and do** according to all that is written in it. For then you shall make your way prosperous, and then you shall deal wisely and have good success.

The first time I read this scripture, I thought "Well that's Old Testament, and under the law, so that doesn't apply to me now." Boy! Was I sadly mistaken. The Lord began to open my understanding so that I could see beyond the Old Testament, to the Lord Jesus Christ and receive what was being conveyed here. I had to understand that in the Old Testament Jesus is concealed; He is revealed in the New Testament so the text does apply to me. I learned that if I observe and do all that the Holy Spirit is leading me to do, and obey the words of the Lord Jesus Christ, I would make my way prosperous and have good success. That is enough to grow some "sure 'nuf" faith. Sure enough to see me through all that God has called me to do. All I have to do is obey the word of God and be an actual DO-er of the word as James admonishes us in James 1:22 *But be doers of the Word [obey the message], and not merely listeners to it, betraying yourselves [into deception by reasoning contrary to the Truth].*

CHAPTER 1 – JESUS FAITH

As Christians *On Assignment*, we must first have faith. Not just any faith, or faith in anything, any person, or our ability, but faith in our savior the Lord Jesus Christ. The book of Hebrews has a lot to say about faith, for instance without faith it is impossible to please God (Hebrews 11:6), and that faith is the substance of things hoped for and the evidence of things not seen (Hebrews 11:1), that we must mix what we hear and learn with faith (Hebrews 4:2), that we hold firm to the faith we profess (Hebrews 4:14), we are told to imitate the faith of those who believed God (Hebrews 6:12), we are told to live by faith (Hebrews 10:38), not to mention there is a wall of faith in Hebrews 11 of men and women who 'by faith' accomplished great *assignments*. My point is to define the meaning of faith for the Christian disciple today, because over the last few years faith has been misunderstood, therefore hindering our ability to walk obediently and with the power and authority we should walk in.

11.4 Defining faith

A definition I stumbled across in the amplified bible of "faith is the leaning of your whole personality on God in complete trust and confidence" (1 Thessalonians 3:7). This definition removes the bulk of faith off of the believer and onto Jesus, our only job is to believe. Speaking of believe, I was taught that a person's beliefs are formed and shaped by an accumulation of information that we base, or root, our beliefs in. So the more information accumulated, the stronger the belief. This can work for positive as well as negative beliefs, yet my *assignment* in this project is to form positive beliefs based on the word of God – helping transform our minds with the word (as in Romans 12:2). The remainder of this chapter will look at faith a little closer and show a direct correlation between faith in Jesus and our ability to walk obediently in the authority He has given us.

> (Mark 11:12-14) On the day following, when they had come away from Bethany, He was hungry. [13] And seeing in the distance a fig tree [covered] with leaves, He went to see if He could find any [fruit] on it [for in the fig tree the fruit appears at the same time as the leaves]. But when He came up to it, He found nothing but leaves, for the fig season had not yet come. [14] And He said to it, No one ever again shall eat fruit from you. And His disciples were listening [to what He said].

> (Mark 11: 20-23 – emphasis added) In the morning, when they were passing along, they noticed that the fig tree was withered [completely] away to its roots. [21] And Peter remembered and said to Him, Master, look! The fig tree which You doomed has withered away! [22] And Jesus, replying, said to them, **HAVE FAITH IN GOD [CONSTANTLY]**. [23] Truly I tell you, whoever says to this mountain, Be lifted up and thrown into the sea! And **DOES NOT DOUBT AT ALL IN HIS HEART** BUT <u>**BELIEVES**</u> that what he says will take place, it will be done for him.

1.2   *Faith and beliefs*

Several observations can be made from this text about authority and the faith that Jesus refers to. In verse 22 Jesus says to have faith in God, not in our ability or training, our knowledge, our own understanding, but in God. The amplified bible takes it a step further and adds "constantly" – it is not enough to have faith in God in the midst of one situation or maybe a few mild situations, but forget about the object of your faith when things get larger and louder than you are accustomed to.

Faith in God is not positive thinking. Yes, you will have to rid yourself of negative thinking, but thinking good thoughts alone and apart from the "in God" part, and His character and ability backing your faith is also needed.

1.3 Faith and doubt
Then in verse 23 we are warned not to doubt in our heart. Personally I thought I understood doubt, but over the course of the past few years I have a better understanding of the term. Beginning with the regular dictionary definition of doubt: fear; suspect; distrust; to lack confidence in; to consider unlikely. We can draw common conclusions from this definition as to what we cannot have in our heart. But looking further at the Strong's definition of doubt: discriminate; to prefer; to withdraw from one, desert; to separate one's self in a hostile spirit, to oppose, strive with dispute, contend – so we can see that doubt enters many areas in our thinking that will be a hindrance to true faith.

This term is translated 19 times in the King James Version as doubt, judge, discern, contend, waver. So digesting these two definitions and the translations of the term, Jesus is telling us to not separate ourselves in a hostile spirit from our faith in God, but to continue to believe Him. Also notice that we are told to not doubt in heart, it is all about the heart, not head/emotions/intellect – but heart. One of my mentors said "you cannot keep birds from flying over your head, but you can stop them from making nests" which means you cannot stop the enemy from firing his fiery darts of doubt, but you can choose to quench those fiery darts with the shield of faith as in Ephesians 6:16.

Casting down every thought that exalts itself above the knowledge of God (2 Corinthians 10:5)... so it is not just thinking positive apart from God, there must be a growing knowledge of God to do as the amplified says and have faith in God continually.

Mark 11:23 says "does not doubt at all in his heart BUT BELIEVES" – the beliefs should be rooted and grounded in God – Jesus – the Holy Spirit...in short, in the Triune God. We will come back to this term after explaining a few more texts about this faith in God and the authority that Jesus brings us and empowers us with.

> (Luke 4:31-37) And He descended to Capernaum, a town of Galilee, and there He continued to teach the people on the Sabbath days. [32] And they were amazed at His teaching, for **His word was with authority and ability and weight and power.** [33] Now in the synagogue there was a man who was possessed by the foul spirit of a demon; and he cried out with a loud (deep, terrible) cry, [34] Ah, let us alone! What have You to do with us [What have we in common], Jesus of Nazareth? Have You come to destroy us? I know Who You are—the Holy One of God! [35] But Jesus rebuked him, saying, Be silent (muzzled, gagged), and come out of him! And when the demon had thrown the man down in their midst, he came out of him without injuring him in any possible way. [36] And they were all amazed and said to one another, What kind of talk is this? For with authority and power He commands the foul

spirits and they come out! [37] And a rumor about Him spread into every place in the surrounding country.

1.4 Faith and authority

As we can see in verse 32 above that through the constant and continual communion with Jesus we grow more and more in the knowledge of His word so that we speak with authority, ability, and power as Jesus did. Not only speak with it, but it will be recognized by others, religious people as well as demons because in verse 34 the demon identified Jesus. And as we get down to verse 36 they were all amazed – this authority will 'amaze' people and bring lies and persecution. This is why we must stay in communion with our Source of power and authority to not be sidetracked or distracted by the 'rumors' that will arise because of the authority that is openly displayed.

Another observation about the authority of Jesus in this text is in verse 35, He did not have a long drawn out conversation with this demon, or draw attention to what He was about to do, or had done – He just did what He came to do as He stated earlier in Luke 4:18 – actually, lets look back a few verses to put in context how we got here in verse 31-37.

> (Luke 4:18-22 NIV) "The Spirit of the Lord is on me, because he has anointed me to preach good news to the poor. He has sent me to proclaim freedom for the prisoners and recovery of sight for the blind, to release the oppressed, [19] to proclaim the year of the Lord's favor." [20] Then he rolled up the scroll, gave it back to the attendant and sat down. The eyes of everyone in the synagogue were fastened on him, [21] and he began by saying to

> them, "Today this scripture is fulfilled in your hearing." ²² All spoke well of him and **were amazed** at the gracious words that came from his lips. "**Isn't this Joseph's son?**" they asked.

So the demon power in verse 34 *believed* more than those that were around in amazement and causing rumors! Now if this is apparent for Jesus, those whom are "*On Assignment*" should not expect any less. Just know like Jesus that there is a purpose for why we have this authority and it is to preach the gospel (the kingdom) and to proclaim good news. No need to respond to the 'amazed' people – just accomplish the *Assignments* set forth from the Lord.

I have a few more examples from the book of Luke that demonstrates the faith and authority that Jesus would like for each of us *"On Assignment"* to possess.

> (Luke 7:1-9) After Jesus had finished all that He had to say in the hearing of the people [on the mountain], He entered Capernaum. ² Now a centurion had a bond servant who was held in honor and highly valued by him, who was sick and at the point of death. ³ And when the **centurion heard of Jesus**, *he sent some Jewish elders* to Him, requesting Him to come and make his bond servant well. ⁴ And when they reached Jesus, they begged Him earnestly, saying, *He is worthy* that You should do this for him, ⁵ For he loves our nation and he built us our synagogue [at his own expense].

⁶ And Jesus went with them. But when He was not far from the house, the **centurion sent [some] friends to Him**, saying, Lord, do not trouble [Yourself], for *I am not sufficiently worthy* to have You come under my roof; ⁷ *Neither did I consider myself worthy to come to You.* But [just] speak a word, and my servant boy will be healed. ⁸ For I also am a man [daily] subject to authority, with soldiers under me. And I say to one, Go, and he goes; and to another, Come, and he comes; and to my bond servant, Do this, and he does it. ⁹ Now when Jesus heard this, He marveled at him, and He turned and said to the crowd that followed Him, I tell you, not even in [all] Israel have I found such **great faith** [as this].

Notice that the centurion's initial faith grew and began as he "heard" of Jesus in verse 4. The text doesn't give explicit details about the sending of the Jewish elders – but in meditating on it, I heard this: the Jewish elders told him of Jesus, but they went forward with their own plea in verse 4-5 about how *worthy* he was to have Jesus come to him – this was their request, not the centurion's because as he pondered on it he sent some friends in verse 6-8 to deliver the real message of his heart. SIDENOTE on friends: Proverbs 17:17 says that (a friend loves at all times, and is born, as is a brother, for adversity) so it is a wise thing to have these types of friends around you that can communicate your heart, and not their desires for you.

Back to the text in Luke 7:1-9, Jesus heard of the centurion's true understanding of authority and how he had a revelation of faith in Jesus (similar to that of Peter and building the church... in Matthew 16:16 & 18) and the authority that

Jesus possessed to create and heal with His words. This was Jesus' heart examination of faith with corresponding actions – not because the centurion was worthy but because of who Jesus is, who the centurion perceived Him to be.

Speaking of Peter and faith – Jesus later prayed that his faith fail not.

> (Luke 22:31-32) Simon, Simon (Peter), listen! Satan has asked excessively that [all of] you be given up to him [out of the power and keeping of God], that he might sift [all of] you like grain, ³² But I have prayed especially for you [Peter], that your [own] **faith may not fail**; and when you yourself have turned again, strengthen and establish your brethren.

So Jesus could see great faith in the centurion, and He could see that at times our faith would be tested, and not just for the purpose of ourselves, but to bring future strengthening for the brethren. Notice that Jesus did not pray for all of Peter, although the amplified makes a distinction that satan asked to sift ALL of him, Jesus only prayed for his faith because he knew that the enemy could not stand against true faith in God.

To tie this into a personal experience, I had been *On Assignment* for some time, had been following the instructions as closely as I could, but the enemy launched a sneak attack and bombardment against me. Things that appeared to be truth proved to be fallacy and the enemy was having a field day. He began to taunt me and make fun of my 'so called faith' and ability to hear and follow God – let me tell you it was not a nice fight. But listening to a commentary on this Luke 22:31-32 by Vernon McGee helped me see a constant truth here, Jesus knew in the text that Peter would deny Him, yet persisted in praying that Peter's faith fail not. So applying this concept to the personal experiences that we will encounter, no matter how the enemy launches those fiery darts – quench them with knowing that Jesus prayed for your faith. Yes, it is good to have a friend pray for me, and to have proven intercessors pray for me, but to know that Jesus prayed (past tense) for me, and is ever praying for me in heaven as my High Priest, interceding on my behalf...that is enough to make you want to shout and run around the room giving God all the glory!!!

1.5   The triune God

I would like to conclude this chapter as promised earlier discussing a little about the Triune God and how having a better understanding of the characteristics of God will strengthen our faith. God the Father; God the Son; God the Holy Spirit. This strengthening will bring on a stronger sense of authority in our lives. The word trinity or triune does not appear in the bible, but the principle and concept are present. It is to our Father who is in Heaven that we pray; it is in the name (authority, nature) of Jesus that we pray; and we have the help of the Holy Spirit in prayer. Allow me to discuss each aspect a little.

God the Father – Our Father in heaven

As Jesus was teaching His disciples to pray in Matthew 6 (the model prayer), He began stating that the Father is in heaven.

God the Son – Pray in His name

It is Jesus giving the instructions in Matthew 6. I also heard that we do not use His name like a stamp we stick on the end of prayer, but requesting in His name that which is in His nature and authority to bring to pass.

God the Holy Spirit – our Helper

He is our helper in prayer in Romans 8:26-28; He is our promised helper in John chapters 14-16.

We see the three at work together at the baptism of Jesus: Jesus is in the water, the Father speaks from heaven, the Holy Spirit descends. Yet another reference to the trinity is in Genesis 1:26 when God said "let us make man in our image." Another way of saying triune God is the godhead – God in three persons: Father, Son, Holy Spirit. When you look at the godhead, it is God consisting of three persons, yet all equal in function. In my studies, I found that the word God is plural, like the word team or marriage. So God is like a team of 3 people. This reference to Genesis 1:26, when the bible says "let us", the "us" here is plural and denotes Elohim, which is a plural team. Here are a few more scriptures that show the triune God:

> (1 John 5:7) So there are three witnesses in heaven: the Father, the Word and the Holy Spirit, and these three are One.

> (2 Corinthians 13:14) The grace (favor and spiritual blessing) of the Lord Jesus Christ and the love of God and the presence and fellowship (the communion and sharing together, and participation) in the Holy Spirit be with you all. Amen (so be it).

> (Acts 2:33) Being therefore lifted high by and to the right hand of God, and having received from the Father the promised [blessing which is the] Holy Spirit, He has made this outpouring which you yourselves both see and hear.

> (Acts 10:38) How God anointed and consecrated Jesus of Nazareth with the

> [Holy] Spirit and with strength and ability and power; how He went about doing good and, in particular, curing all who were harassed and oppressed by [the power of] the devil, for God was with Him.

The triune God, the 28ettingd, or the trinity, whatever you refer to, it is not theological, but practical. You can tell from the above 4 scripture references, the three work together as one, with different roles, functions and characteristics. The Holy Spirit does not override Jesus (the word of God), they work in unison for the purpose of the Father. We know that Jesus is our Savior, and we now live in a time when we really need to implore the help of the Holy Spirit to fulfill each and every *assignment*. The Holy Spirit is not a force, or a power, but a powerful person that is our Helper – He is not an "it", but a person. Here is a list of some of the activities of the Holy Spirit: He teaches, guides, comforts, helps our infirmities, intercedes for the saints, searches the deep things of God, and so much more.

CHAPTER 2 – ON ASSIGNMENT

2.1 *How do I know?*

Honestly, I am not sure how to tell you exactly how you will know what your *assignment* is. To tell the truth, this was a very difficult chapter for me to address because I don't feel qualified to spell out the "How Do I Know" process. Yet I do qualify to be obedient and write what I am hearing the Lord lead me to write. I have gathered some ideas together, and now I simply yield my members to the Holy Spirit to write through me.

A place to begin is to make sure that you have a true grasp of all that salvation really is. For me, I was saved in 1988 received Jesus as my Savior but did not recognize and understand the Lordship *portion* of salvation and all that it contained until 1998. I knew that I was saved, but I knew nothing of how to grow in the direction God desired for me. I thank God that He never leaves you alone, and He has sent His Holy Spirit to be our teacher on the inside (1 John 2:27). Once I was exposed to the fact that you can have a personal relationship with the Lord, my entire outlook changed on attending church and reading my bible.

2.2 *Self evaluations*

>(Psalm 68:19 KJV) Blessed be the Lord, who daily loadeth us with benefits, even the God of our salvation. Selah.

>(Psalm 68:19-20 AMP) Blessed be the Lord, Who bears our burdens and carries us day by day, even the God Who is our salvation! Selah [pause, and calmly think of that]! God is to us a **God of deliverances and salvation**;

and to God the Lord belongs escape from death [setting us free].

Allow me to take you on a journey to further understand this reference to Psalm 68 by looking at the seven churches in Revelation chapters 2 and chapter 3. These churches were either warned or commended for their spiritual progress. It would be a good step to regularly read through these chapters and see where we are. The following is an outline to show you what I am referring to, to help assist you in your routine self-evaluation. And remember, it is never too late, He states that "he who has an ear to hear, let him hear." As soon as you are aware of what you have not been hearing, listen to it and take heed with actions following. There is a difference between hearing and listening; hearing acquires information, and maybe even agrees with it, but it is not shown that you listened until you do something with the information received.

Ephesus (the loveless church) Revelation 2:1-7

They had lost their zeal for the love of God, and the things of God. Talking about the responsive love, not agape love (responding to Him in *obedience*). They were warned to repent or He would remove His lamp stand (light) from them. **Evaluation:** Is your love for God still hot?

Smyrna (the persecuted church) Revelation 2:8-17

They were commended for living through persecution and tribulation. They were also notified that the persecution and tribulation would continue as long as they walked in the light. The stated time of the 10 days was to assure them that although these situations would arise, they are not lifelong. **Evaluation:** Are you being persecuted? Endure!

Pergamos (the compromising church) Revelation 2:12-17

They were warned because some held the doctrine of Balaam (see Numbers 22-25). A brief description of this doctrine is that Balaam was once a prophet of God, yet he was led astray by the lust of the flesh, greed, self-gain, seeking a reward rather than *obedience.* He taught the enemies of God how to corrupt God's people. To quote Reverend Brian McCallum, *"The doctrine of Balaam is to do whatever it takes to get what you want—to use whatever God gave you to get yourself gain ... The deeds of the Nicolaitanes ... they were loose and careless in the way they lived in the natural, and they elevated the clergy or ministers above the people they ministered to."* Basically, they compromised because they tolerated things they should not have. They were warned to repent quickly. **Evaluation:** Do you do as unto the Lord or men? Do you compromise your core values for gain? Do you elevate man over God? What are you tolerating that is contrary to the word of God (in your life and your church)?

Thyatira (the corrupt church) Revelation 2:18-29

Thyatira was a small thriving business city (of craftsmen and tradesmen) that sometimes put pressure on people to take a stand for righteousness and not give in to pagan ways. Jezebel taught them to live carelessly and immorally; anyway that they wanted. She was given time to repent, and we are too if we find ourselves here. **Evaluation:** Do you let enterprise and business sway your beliefs and morals? Are you pursuing holiness, or careless and immoral living?

Sardis (the dead church) Revelation 3:1-6

This city was once the wealthiest city in all Asia. Wealthy but degenerate because they were trying to live on their past reputation. NO. *Be ye Doers of the word, not REMEMBERS only*. They were warned to be watchful and strengthen the things that remained. **Evaluation:** Are you in need of personal revival/ strengthening/ refreshment to stay alive? Have there been any new revelations/illuminations to you since your last evaluation? If not, seek God now…

Philadelphia (the faithful church) Revelation 3:7-13

They were keeping His word and did not deny His name; they were admonished to hold fast. When your works are committed to the Lord, your light is renewed. Yet this church was the youngest of the 7 churches listed. **Evaluation:** Are you holding fast to your confession of faith? Are you ever declaring His name and keeping His word?

Laodiceans (the lukewarm church) Revelation 3:14-22

They were the only church of the 7 that did not receive a commendation prior to their message. Meaning there was *nothing* to commend them on. They were also a very wealthy center of trade, finance, banking, and investment. They were neither cold nor hot— signifying spiritual poverty which can be defined as trusting in riches instead of the Lord God. They were not actually relying on God to sustain them because they were physically comfortable. **<u>Evaluation:</u>** Does your own ability keep you from totally trusting God? God never meant for us to be comfortable and not reach out to others – we never "arrive" in this realm.

Learn to yield to the inner warnings of the Holy Spirit. No longer press past those danger signs and act like you didn't see or hear them— and then play shocked when the preacher calls you out across the pulpit (when it seems like his message is aimed directly at you). We are to take heed to these warnings because the purpose is to bring us into being overcomers. A good book to help you understand this subject further is titled "Seven Letters To Seven Churches— Breaking The Bread Of Revelation Volume Two" by Brian McCallum (1989).

The Spirit of the Lord is showing us a laundry list of the church's (body of Christ) weaknesses and strengths. We are to make sure that we examine ourselves (it is an individual duty) and wash ourselves with the water of the word of God; creating a strong, renewed mind— the mind of Christ. A good reminder to go through this self-evaluation and examination is the monthly observance of communion. One of the communion text often used is found in 1 Corinthians 11; and the text tells us to examine ourselves.

After studying these 7 churches in the book of Revelation, we now can refer back to Psalm 68:20, the amplified bible reads *"God is to us a **God of deliverances and salvation.**"* So we can see that we are saved, salvation is ours, yet we rely on God to help us through deliverance after deliverance from habits that we find in ourselves. These monthly examinations help us discover areas that God is working on us in. Notice salvation is singular, it only takes one time, and deliverance is plural so we see that the deliverance *portion* may take place over and over again. Also, in the King James Version of Psalm 68:19 it reads: *Blessed be the Lord, who daily loadeth us with **benefits**, even the God of our salvation* – benefits is plural – so these deliverances and benefits can come daily. Thank You Lord! We grow from faith to faith, and glory to glory.

2.3 *Work out your salvation*
Okay, now we have a better understanding of salvation and our daily benefits, but that still isn't telling me my individual *"assignment"*? I know. I'm working my way into that. First base was for you to get a better understanding of salvation. Now second base is to teach you how to **work out your own salvation.** The next text reference will explain this:

> (Philippians 2:12) Therefore, my dear ones, as you have always obeyed [my suggestions], so now, not only [with the enthusiasm you would show] in my presence but much more because I am absent, **work out (cultivate, carry out to the goal, and fully complete) your own salvation** with reverence and awe and trembling (self-distrust, with serious caution, tenderness of conscience, watchfulness against temptation, timidly shrinking from whatever might offend God and discredit the name of Christ).

This may sound easier said than done, just remember it is a process that does not happen overnight – it requires much "working" to obtain. Please do not confuse working *out* your salvation with the twisted doctrine of working *for* your salvation. Salvation is a done deal in Christ. The "work out" part of this text is the process of renewing your mind, going from faith to faith and glory to glory – actually living the word, getting a proven track record of submitting yourself to God and resisting the devil so he will flee, and so on and so on – just so you can get the picture of what I mean.

2.4 & 2.5 *Intimacy with God*

A good third base in knowing or seeking your *assignment* is to increase your understanding of intimacy with God.

IN – TO – ME – SEE = intimacy.

Not intimacy in a derogatory way in which the world sometime uses the word, but a growing understanding of the characteristics of God, understanding the various names of God, just continued hunger and thirst for God that He promised He would supply. This intimacy is growing up spiritually – true intimacy. My spiritual growth is attributed to being hungry for more; it is good to attain more and reach goals, but never be satisfied, always stay in the flow. Another byproduct from spiritual growth is a better understanding of anointing. I do not profess to be a bible scholar, I just know a lot about the bible and the Author of it and desire to know even more. I found an entry in one of my spiritual growth journals that said "this is a product of a painful situation…and then to be misunderstood adds to the pain." Not all parts of your individual growth process will be understood by those around you – just know that God understands. One of the purposes for this I found, was to increase our thirst for knowledge and understanding by (from) God – which is another byproduct of the painful situations we experience. To quote the motto of a school I attend here in Houston: The Call Is Free, The Gift Is By Grace, The Mantle Will Cost. Yes, I have truly been living this motto on various levels over the past 21 years.

One body, many members as in 1 Corinthians 12, I am part of the feet. The feet do more work, it is normal, but the feet are sometimes taken for granted…I am called with an anointing to clean fish (yes catch them and administrate, but the call is on discipleship). As I read this statement about feet, I am now facing a weight challenge of being 20 pounds overweight, which causes my feet and knees to be sore at the end of the day. The added weight is also causing a side effect of high cholesterol and hypertension. Stay with me, I will tie this into the topic of it all working together. The importance of <u>YOUR</u> purpose is so great because it is causing weight on the other parts that are in line with God's purpose; added issues that would not be so if all the members were in alignment. Yes saved, attending church, growing spiritually – that is equated to all this exercise and learning how the body functions, adjusting my diet and sleep patterns; my desired goal in doing these is better health and stamina to fulfill the will of God for my life. Is that not the goal of the body of Christ? To fulfill "thy kingdom come, thy will be <u>done</u>" it will require some action and preparation on our part. Work it out – walk it out. Good, healthy bodies, naturally and spiritually.

Prayerfully by the time this book goes to print, I will have lost 12 of this 20 pounds (my doctor's goal). Wouldn't that be something if the entire body of Christ could distribute it's weight as such?!?! That is a 60% improvement! Will you be a part of this?

2.6   Hunger and thirst for God

Our hungering and thirsting for God should never be satisfied. Yes, He will be your Manna from heaven and wells/rivers of living water, but the instructions in the Old Testament for manna was a daily instruction – to gather what was needed for each day (see Exodus 16). We can say a day is a time period in life, therefore throughout each time period (day) in our lifetime, we should be gathering manna and drinking from the wells of living water.

Another aspect of knowing your *assignment* is the pure word of God. He is the Creator of all things and has given us several scriptures to help lead, guide and direct us. In this next section I will just list a few texts that helped me get in the proper direction He has for me, pausing to make a few comments in between.

> (Jeremiah 29:11-13) For I know the thoughts and plans that I have for you, says the Lord, thoughts and plans for welfare and peace and not for evil, to give you hope in your final outcome. [12] Then you will call upon Me, and you will come and pray to Me, and I will hear and heed you. [13] Then you will seek Me, inquire for, and require Me [as a vital necessity] and find Me when you search for Me with all your heart.

Not only does God have us in thought, He has prepared a plan, it is up to us to seek Him for the plan. Also keep in mind that our thoughts are not His thoughts – He is coming from a level that we don't fully understand, yet His words have creative power so we need to be saying what God says.

> (Isaiah 55:8, 11) For My thoughts are not your thoughts, neither are your ways My ways, says the Lord. ... [11] So shall My word be that goes forth out of My mouth: it shall not return to Me void [without producing any effect, useless], but it shall accomplish that which I please and purpose, and it shall prosper in the thing for which I sent it.

Call unto Him again…

> (Jeremiah 33:2-3) Thus says the Lord Who made [the earth], the Lord Who formed it to establish it—the Lord is His name: **[3] Call to Me and I will answer you** and show you great and mighty things, fenced in and hidden, which you do not know (do not distinguish and recognize, have knowledge of and understand).

At times things may not seem like they are going right, it may appear that everything is going all wrong. Just make sure that you are faithful to do your part (which will be discussed a little further in the next section) and keep this text in mind…

> (Romans 8:28) We are assured and know that [God being a partner in their labor] all things work together and are [fitting into a plan] for

good to and for those who love God and are called according to [His] design and purpose.

Our biblical friend Joseph has a lot to say about how these things are working together for our good…

> (Genesis 45:4-8, verse 5 is the key) And Joseph said to his brothers, Come near to me, I pray you. And they did so. And he said, I am Joseph your brother, whom you sold into Egypt! **⁵ But now, do not be distressed and disheartened or vexed and angry with yourselves because you sold me here, for God sent me ahead of you to preserve life.** ⁶ For these two years the famine has been in the land, and there are still five years more in which there will be neither plowing nor harvest. ⁷ God sent me before you to preserve for you a posterity and to continue a remnant on the earth, to save your lives by a great escape and save for you many survivors. ⁸ So now it was not you who sent me here, but God; and He has made me a father to Pharaoh and lord of all his house and ruler over all the land of Egypt.

2.7 Desire…

A great text that can help with the "how do I know" of your *assignment* is Psalm 37. The entire book is a good read, so when you get a moment read over it in it's entirety – and go ahead and look at Psalm 73 because they both say the same thing generally. We will just look at 2 verses:

> (Psalm 37:3-5 NIV) Trust in the LORD and do good; dwell in the land and enjoy safe pasture. [4] Delight yourself in the LORD and he will give you the desires of your heart. [5] Commit your way to the LORD; trust in him and he will do this:

A key to desire and the fulfillment is trusting God, as in verse 3. Trust is faith in God. I heard someone say "you don't have any problem, all you need is faith in God" and this is so true. Verse 4, the desires of your heart – we will have to learn to listen to our heart because that is where He lives. Heart is spirit, and that is where the Holy Spirit resides – yet in my studies, I found that the heart is in both the spirit realm and the soul realm. The best example that I can think of is found in Psalm 51:10 when David cries out to God to create in him a new heart and renew a right spirit. See section 4.3, dealing with the heart, to better see this point.

Also, make sure that your delight is in the law of the Lord, not anything else. No, I'm not being legalistic with the law as we in the United States think of it, law is God's ways of doing things; and the number one law is LOVE.

> (Psalm 37:23-24 NIV) If the LORD delights in a man's way, he makes his steps firm; [24] though he stumble, he will not fall, for the LORD upholds him with his hand.

In seeking God and following His instructions, we can draw these points when the Lord actually delights in us as in Psalm 37 above: 1) He makes our way firm, 2) even when we fall He will uphold us.

2.8 What type of vessel are you?

> (2 Tim 2:20-22) So whoever cleanses himself [from what is ignoble and unclean, who separates himself from contact with contaminating and corrupting influences] will [then himself] be a vessel set apart and useful for honorable and noble purposes, consecrated and profitable to the Master, fit and ready for any good work.
>
> [22] Shun youthful lusts and flee from them, and aim at and pursue righteousness (all that is virtuous and good, right living, conformity to the will of God in thought, word, and deed); [and aim at and pursue] faith, love, [and] peace (harmony and concord with others) in fellowship with all [Christians], who call upon the Lord out of a pure heart.

There are two types of vessels discussed here in this text. I want to take a few moments to discuss the vessel options that we have: of noble and honorable use, or of ignoble and dishonorable use? As I studied this text I found that my understanding of noble and ignoble had to be expanded. See the following Merriam-Webster dictionary definitions:

> Noble: Possessing outstanding qualities; illustrious; famous; notable; grand or impressive especially in appearance; moral.
>
> Ignoble: Characterized by baseness, lowness, or meanness; mean.
> Mean: To design for or destine to a specified purpose of future; to have in mind as a purpose; intend; humble.

So it is not a negative thing to be an ignoble vessel, the issue is about being clean and unclean; as well as useful and un-useful. To help better illustrate this point, I will share what I found describing vessels from a Dictionary of Biblical Types by Walter L Wilson:

> All kinds of vessels are necessary in the house of God. Some are very fancy, delicate, expensive, and more ornamental than useful. Such is the beautiful vase that adorns the mantle in the parlor. It represents the attractive gold, cut glass or ornamental pieces that beautify the parlor of the home. There are other vessels, however, which are called vessels of dishonor. These are the kitchen utensils, the skillet, the pans, the coffee pot. Most folks would like to be the golden ornament in the parlor, but those in the kitchen are more useful. The purging from "these" is not purging the golden vessels from the kitchen vessels, it refers to purging oneself from the evils mentioned in the previous part of the chapter. If one does this, then the Lord can use him wherever He wishes, perhaps in the parlor, or perhaps in the kitchen. He will be subject to the will of his Lord.

That of itself is a mouthful. So will you be a vessel that the master can use? A pretty vase can be sat on a mantle and bring beauty to a room, yet the same vase doubles into a trash can that can keep the room clean. So which vessel will you be? The choice is yours. It lies in your *obedience* to separate yourself from contact with contaminating and corrupting influences as the text says – and to walk a consecrated life that is profitable unto the master. See section 8.4 for more information on the consecrated life.

Shunning youthful lust is a personal act that will require maturing in the things of God. To shun means to put off, to flee from; the Merriam-Webster dictionary defines shun as: to avoid deliberately and especially habitually; and a synonym is escape. So shunning will require a person to have deliberate and habitual actions toward righteousness; which the amplified bible describes as all that is virtuous and good, right living, conformity to the will of God in thought, word, and deed – all of which require a deliberate action on our part. The most important deliberate action is learning/ acquiring/ getting the will of God for our lives which in turn empowers us to walk in it and be a useful vessel for the Master, whether of noble or ignoble use, the choice is up to the Master.

In being a useful vessel, you will face persecution and trial and be targeted for malice by the adversary – this is why it is so important to know your goal and your purpose up front so that you remain clean and useful. There is a not so obvious example of what I am speaking of in Daniel chapter 5:

> (Daniel 5:2-3) Belshazzar, while he was tasting the wine, commanded that the gold and silver vessels which his father Nebuchadnezzar had taken out of the temple [out of the sacred area—the Holy Place and the Holy of Holies] whi— was in Jerusalem be brought, that the king and his lords, his wives, and his concubines might drink from them. ³ Then they brought in the gold and silver vessels which had been taken out of the temple, the house of God which was in Jerusalem; and the king and his lords, his wives, and his concubines drank from them.

Daniel chapter 5 is better explained in Daniel chapter 1, then you will understand why I say that being a vessel meet for the Master's use will bring persecution and trials:

> (Daniel 1:2-6) And the Lord gave Jehoiakim king of Judah into his hand, along with a part of the vessels of the house of God; and he carried them into the land of Shinar [Babylonia] to the house of his god and placed the vessels in the treasury of his god. ³ And the [Babylonian] king told Ashpenaz, the master of his eunuchs, to bring in some of the children of Israel, both of the royal family and of the nobility— ⁴ youths without blemish, well-favored in appearance and skillful in all wisdom, discernment, and understanding, apt in learning knowledge, competent to stand and serve in the king's palace—and to teach them the literature and language of the Chaldeans. ⁵ And the king assigned for them a daily *portion* of his own rich and dainty food and of the wine which he drank. They were to be so educated and so nourished for three years that at the end of that time they might stand before the king. ⁶ Among these were of the children of Judah: Daniel, Hananiah, Mishael, and Azariah.

Survey the book of Daniel and notice all the trials that these 4 Hebrew boys endured. Yet they always landed in a favorable position with God – this is our assignment today – to be obedient to God through whatever comes our way and be an example to the world that has no regard for God. Some of you may be on a job where it appears like they are doing you as Daniel chapter 1:4, take a second and re-read that verse above…it is a set up for your personal refiner's fire testing to prove your faith which is more precious than God. See these next 4 strings of scripture to better illustrate this point:

> (Malachi 3:2-3) But who can endure the day of His coming? And who can stand when He appears? For He is like a refiner's fire and like fullers' soap; ^{3} He will sit as a refiner and purifier of silver, and He will purify the priests, the sons of Levi, and refine them like gold and silver, that they may offer to the Lord offerings in righteousness.
>
> (1 Peter 4:6-7) [You should] be exceedingly glad on this account, though now for a little while you may be distressed by trials and suffer temptations, ^{7} So that [the genuineness] of your faith may be tested, [your faith] which is infinitely more precious than the perishable gold which is tested and purified by fire. [This proving of your faith is intended] to redound to [your] praise and glory and honor when Jesus Christ (the Messiah, the Anointed One) is revealed.
>
> (Psalm 66:10) For You, O God, have proved us; You have tried us as silver is tried, refined, and purified.
>
> (Psalm 48:10) Behold, I have refined you, but not as silver; I have tried and chosen you in the furnace of affliction.

The silver and gold referred to in these last two texts can be explained even further. Silver can refer figuratively to the testing of human hearts; and wisdom is declared to be more valuable than silver. Hence the wisdom of the word of God being so vital to the Christian that desires to be a vessel meet for the Master's use. Another fact that I found in studying the use of silver in the bible is that it refers to redemption, which is the foundation of the sinner's safety and standing. Also notice that we do not read about silver being in heaven because there is no need for redemption there – the streets are paved with gold.

Gold in biblical days was valued and used because of its beauty and workability. The refiner could heat up and mold gold into various things. The purification process is what the walk of *obedience* does for the *Christian on Assignment.*

So what type of vessel are you? Useful? Or crusted and of no use to the Master? Still possessing the dross that the fire of trials came to separate and remove? Or shining bright and reflective as silver and gold were meant to do? I have yet a few more vessels to discuss in this section before moving on.

A scriptural example of both a clean (useful) vessel and a vessel that is not "meet for the Master's use" is found in Matthew 25 of the 10 virgins. Half were termed "wise" and the other half were termed "foolish" – which is another way of saying useful and un-useful.

> (Matthew 25:1-5 NKJV) Then the kingdom of heaven shall be likened to ten virgins who took their lamps and went out to meet the bridegroom. [2] Now five of them were wise, and five were foolish. [3] Those who were foolish took their lamps and took no oil with them, [4] but the wise took oil in their vessels with their lamps. [5] But while the bridegroom was delayed, they all slumbered and slept.

The prepared virgins brought their vessels that contained the oil for the lamp. Psalms states that the word of God is a guide unto my feet and a light unto my pathway; what was needed was light, but with no oil this is not possible. A comment that I found in studying this further is "The 5 wise were really in touch with heaven and all of God's supply of the Spirit. The other 5 had simply been worked UPON by the Spirit, whereby certain good results had been obtained, but not that complete act of linking them with heaven and God, called the New Birth." What a shameful state to be exposed to the means to become useful, have the instructions in your possession, but never actually take the time to apply the instructions to become useful; yet many people are like these 5 foolish that know about the coming bridegroom, but never take the needed steps to be ready. Again, I am not referring to working to get saved, but an appreciation for what has been done for you through Christ, so you work the works that will lead to the renewing of the mind to be like Christ.

Marred vessels are not altogether done away with, there is yet hope. See this next biblical example of marred (or unclean, or dirty) vessels that must yield unto the Lord for help:

> (Jeremiah 18:4) And the vessel that he was making from clay was spoiled in the hand of the potter; so he made it over, reworking it into another vessel as it seemed good to the potter to make it.

The best place to be is in the hand of the Potter. Yet we must stay pliable so He will continually add water to our clay to keep it moist and workable; as well as apply constant pressure to us to shape us and mold us into a vessel He can use. God is so in control! The text here in Jeremiah 18 is referencing the mar of the Children of Israel in that they had sinful practices that must be dealt with. It is by the washing of the word of God that these mars can be cleansed away.

God is a good God, and He is a just God as well that must deal with sin in the life of His people (see Romans 9:22-28 for a further example). This is another reason why the self-examinations in section 2.2 are so important, it is part of the washing with the water of the word.

The beauty of these vessels is that even though we may appear to be marred and headed down the wrong road, God is still in control. Even when we are blatantly out of the will of God, He can work things out and is working things out for Himself to get the glory. We are just vessels. Look at the example of Saul, whom we will later know as the Apostle Paul, but this text took place at the beginning of his Christian life, at his conversion while he was on his way to murder Christians thinking he was helping God:

> (Acts 9:15 NKJV) But the Lord said to him, "Go, for he is a chosen vessel of Mine to bear My name before Gentiles, kings, and the children of Israel."

A follow up note for this text in Acts 9 is that God makes the believer the receptacle for the gifts and graces of the Spirit for the use and glory of His great name. Saul went from a murderer of the Christians to a well known traveling evangelist, apostle, and planter of churches whom wrote over half of the books in the New Testament. The proof of this is that Paul went on to write this next text that is his testimony of what he had actively learned from God about becoming a vessel meet for the Master's use – and how this usefulness can land us in what seems like trial after trial, after trial. Yet be encouraged...

> (2 Corinthians 4:7-10) However, we possess this precious treasure [the divine Light of the Gospel] in [frail, human] vessels of earth, that the grandeur and exceeding greatness of the

power may be shown to be from God and not from ourselves. ⁸ We are hedged in (pressed) on every side [troubled and oppressed in every way], but not cramped or crushed; we suffer embarrassments and are perplexed and unable to find a way out, but not driven to despair; ⁹ We are pursued (persecuted and hard driven), but not deserted [to stand alone]; we are struck down to the ground, but never struck out and destroyed; ¹⁰ Always carrying about in the body the liability and exposure to the same putting to death that the Lord Jesus suffered, so that the [resurrection] life of Jesus also may be shown forth by and in our bodies.

Yes, we are mere marred earthen vessels that the Lord is at work in and on. Marred, but in His hand. It may get dry sometimes, continue to wash and water with the water of the word of God because God is calling for pure vessels as mentioned here in:

(1 Thessalonians 4:1-9 NKJV) Finally then, brethren, we urge and exhort in the Lord Jesus that you should abound more and more, just as you received from us how you ought to walk and to please God; ² for you know what commandments we gave you through the Lord Jesus. ³ For this is the will of God, your sanctification: that you should abstain from sexual immorality; ⁴ **that each of you should know how to possess his own vessel in sanctification and honor,** ⁵ not in passion of lust, like the Gentiles who do not know God; ⁶ that no one should take advantage of and defraud his brother in this matter, because the Lord is the avenger of all such, as

we also forewarned you and testified. ⁷ For God did not call us to uncleanness, but in holiness. ⁸ Therefore he who rejects this does not reject man, but God, who has also given us His Holy Spirit.

All of this talk about vessels for the Master's use has been an attempt to alert you to know the direction your *assignment* is in.

2.9 On Assignment— Training/Preparation

I would like to start this section out with a quote from a Mother that I heard in a church I visited. I think her name was Mother Nugent, but she said "You have to get in condition to fit the position." At first this was a straight turn off to me. I immediately thought that she was being caught up in positions in the church. But as she expounded, she was talking about baseball. You have to get in condition to play certain positions in baseball. You can't just say you are the pitcher, you have to train. The same with this "*On Assignment*" training. Yes, God will call you, but He also will equip you. And this takes training, and time.

Like with David, he had been anointed as king at a young age (as a teenager); yet he remained with the sheep, on the backside of the mountain; this was all part of God's training. This training and preparation will take study, much discipline, and trials and persecution to examine if you are ready for the next part of the *assignment*.

> (2 Timothy 2:15) Study and be eager and do your utmost to present yourself to God approved (tested by trial), a workman who

has no cause to be ashamed, correctly analyzing and accurately dividing [rightly handling and skillfully teaching] the Word of Truth.

We must take time and study out the things of God, study the word of Truth for ourselves. I personally don't like for anyone to chew up my food and put it in my mouth. Not now that I am an adult and can eat on my own. Small children think nothing of getting chewed up food, but as they mature they don't care for it. The same is true with God's children spiritually. In the beginning regurgitated food already processed by someone else is okay; meaning it is okay to only receive revelation and illumination from your pastor or other ministers. But as you mature in the things of God, you need to grow in how you receive from God. Maybe begin by taking notes from pastor's messages, or a devotional, or a book you are reading and going back and reading every scripture that was quoted in its entire context. So if he begins at chapter 3 of a book, go back and read chapter 1 – 3 to get a running start of the meaning of the word and the point the person was making. Also study the context in which the scripture was written. And know this, the more you know, the more you realize you don't know – the studying can go on forever – literally. But don't use that as an excuse not to study. I heard a minister on television a few years ago say this "I only minister what I hear. I don't minister what I study. I study to show myself approved, but I don't minister everything I study. I only minister what I hear from the Spirit of God." Now everyone reading this book may not be ministers that will end up on television, but you are a minister within your household and within your circle of influence. You are an epistle that is being read by people, so as you study the word of Truth, you will begin to walk out more of it. So studying is very important to fulfilling the *assignments* of *obedience* in your life.

And know this, as you are studying the word of Truth, you will begin to receive answers for areas that don't even apply to what you are studying. It is just a principle with God, that as you spend time with Him communing in His word and in His presence, you will begin to hear Him clearly in other areas of your life. Give it a try…

I want to share another personal journal entry to help illustrate the importance of communing and studying with God:

> "I thank You Lord for teaching me how to be happy = complete surrender of all to You. And I can actually walk the testimony of 'I can NOT be defeated and I will NOT quit!' Jesus didn't quit, He finished, we are to be molded, shaped, and formed into His likeness and character. Well, first things first, quit is not an option! The only thing I quit is allowing my *personal feelings* to get hurt in this *spiritual battle*! All I have to do is surrender to carry out all that You say and illuminate to me. You even said You'd never give me more than I can bear. So I know that I have Your "stuff" in me to get through and conquer anything I face. Continue to prepare me Lord and illuminate your "stuff" within me. Happy and content – firm in You."

Knowing your *assignment* will require preparation and training which is only achieved by spending time in the word of God.

2.10   Timing and Details

I would just like to share a *Portion* of a prophetic utterance from 8/15/2005 while in a prayer service during a ministry training program I attended:

> Opportunities, opportunities will soon await – some good and some not of the Lord – so it is important that you walk close to Me... go with your spirit, with the nudging in your spirit from Me. Knowing as you walk with Me there shall be an anointing as never before and where there has been struggles, there shall be victory. Stay faithful and know it is just around the corner – so laugh at the devil. Ha, ha, ha, ha... refreshed, renewed taking the path the Lord directs.

This was during a time of seeking the purpose of God. The reason I included this was to show that there will be opportunities that arise that seem like the optimal thing to do on the surface, or at first glance. Yet we must seek the Lord's will with these opportunities. Shortly after I finished the training program, I was entering back into the regular work field. I thought I understood the instructions at the beginning of my training journey, but then 2 ½ years later it appeared that things changed drastically. After much natural seeking and applying for various jobs, I had limited options and directions in which to go. I had two choices, but was unsure as to which was the better decision, the godly decision. So I just wrote out the details of each option and prayed. The option that made the least logical sense is where the peace of God rested. So I went with the not popular choice – after 2 years it was revealed that the other option would have held major restrictions and I would not have had the freedom and opportunities for growth (naturally and spiritually). When I was making the decision, I recalled this prophetic word and included it in my prayer time of making the decision. I will just refer you to chapter 8 on prayer to better understand the role of prayer and choosing the proper opportunities.

We must pay close attention to the instructions that God gives. As I heard a pastor say "the anointing is in the instructions" – and I will add on that the answer is on the other side of *obedience* to the instructions; it isn't always pretty or comfortable, but be obedient. Also know that partial *obedience* is full disobedience. We must remain sensitive to do what He says, when He says it, and how He says to do it.

We must pay attention to the details and follow them. Let me share a personal experience to help illustrate the point here. In 2007 the Lord gave me specific instructions on getting my daughter a vehicle. The instructions were simple and only 2 parts: 1) a 4-door, and 2) no more than $250 per month for the note. Not difficult at all, very general and specific, easy to follow. But wouldn't you know that I missed it majorly! She had her heart set on a Volkswagen Beetle, which only comes in a 2-door. We searched and found one for a *reasonable* price, but it did not meet the instructions of $250 per month. We reasoned with the instructions and said things like "God will provide; and He doesn't mind us having nice stuff". Which were both true statements, but out of context because we had specific instructions. Long story short, we ended up with a 2-door car and a monthly note of $330. Disobedient to the instructions. Only God foreknew that three months later we would have a major life change that would cost exactly $80 per month (the exact difference of $330 – $250) and be very difficult in a 2-door car! Consequences for not following the details… caused us to implore God's grace once we repented for not following ALL of the instructions – but still had to deal with the weight I placed upon myself. I "reasoned" with the instructions in pride and listening to someone else, my daughter, instead of God and His details. Kind of like Eve with her instructions but I was more so the Adam here because I should have stuck to the initial instructions as God gave them to me. It may appear that I have gotten off the subject of timing and details, but do you see how my failure to follow ALL the details hindered the timing of future *assignments* in God because I gave partial and not full *obedience*. The vehicle loan is over a 5 year time span, I am believing God that since I repented, it does not take that long to get back into His timing.

How long O Lord? Galatians 6:9 NLT says: *So let's not get tired of doing what is good.* ***At just the right time*** *we will reap a harvest of blessing if we don't give up.* Just the right time is God's time. We are not in control of the times, but we are in control of choosing to press on in God and not get tired or weary in the process. As discussed earlier, when we push for our own timing we can hinder our overall progress. If we truly trust the Lord and His leading, guiding abilities, we will be found "waiting" on Him for His divine timing. And waiting does not mean sitting idle doing nothing, but like a waiter at a restaurant, to wait upon the kingdom of God in the earth and assist in meeting the needs of the people. You shall reap if you faint not.

2.11   I Won't Complain

Another issue to beware of is murmuring and complaining. Sometimes we may not even feel as if we have entered into this realm, but as we mature in God, His view of what is a complaint or a murmur changes. First, lets define these terms using the Merriam-Webster's dictionary:

> Complain: from a Latin root word which means to lament; to express grief, pain, or discontent; to make a formal accusation or charge. Another root word for complain is "plaint" which comes from a Greek word which means to strike; to beat one's breast, lament; wail; protest.
>
> Murmur: from a Latin root word which means roar; a half-suppressed or muttered complaint; grumbling; an atypical sound of the heart typically indicating a functional or structural abnormality.

So we can see from these definitions that we must be mindful of what is going on in our heart. We must be as the Apostle Paul says, content in whatever state we are in (Philippians 4:11). Complaining is making a formal accusation that God does not really know what He is doing. As the definition goes further, we can see that complaining equates us with a child because only immature children beat their chest when they want something or are not getting their way of how they think things should go. Also, the last part of the murmur definition was interesting to me because it is the term doctors use to note an abnormality with the physical heart (the muscle) – and it is the spiritual heart that God is constantly examining while we go through the various trials and tribulations – it is the heart that is actually getting prepared for the lifelong journey that God has us on of *obedience*. *Obedience* begins in the heart.

Even Jesus realized and lets us see that complaining and murmuring is a stumbling block in John 6:61 AMP — *But Jesus, knowing within Himself that His disciples were complaining and protesting and grumbling about it, said to them: Is this a stumbling block and an offense to you? [Does this upset and displease and shock and scandalize you?]*

The following two texts are a good way that we can shield ourselves from this offense that Jesus detected:

> (Philippians 2:14-15) Do all things without grumbling and faultfinding and complaining [against God] and questioning and doubting [among yourselves], ¹⁵ That you may show yourselves to be blameless and guiltless, innocent and uncontaminated, children of God without blemish (faultless, unrebukable) in the midst of a crooked and wicked generation [spiritually perverted and perverse], among whom you are seen as bright lights (stars or beacons shining out clearly) in the [dark] world

> (1 Peter 4:19) Practice hospitality to one another (those of the household of faith). [Be hospitable, be a lover of strangers, with brotherly affection for the unknown guests, the foreigners, the poor, and all others who come your way who are of Christ's body.] And [in each instance] do it ungrudgingly (cordially and graciously, without complaining but as representing Him)

A note to those in leadership: complaining can cause a lot of people to face the wrath of God. In Joshua 9, Joshua and the leaders made a covenant with the Gibeonites. True, this was done without consulting God on the part of the leaders (see verse 14), and in deceit on the part of the Gibeonites (see verses 4-6), but it was a covenant none-the-less. To leaders, we must make sure that we don't run ahead of God and make decisions without consulting with Him first. It appears that the Gibeonites trusted the hand of God more than the leaders because the Gibeonites knew they were doomed for death according to the news that had come to them in verse 1, so they devised a plan to stay alive based on the zealousness of the leaders and playing on their compassion.

One final note on what murmuring can produce: *But they murmured in their tents and hearkened not to the voice of the Lord (Psalm 106:25).* Murmuring can get you out of the will of God because there is too much noise to listen to His voice. This text, Psalm 106, is telling of Israel's rebelliousness and the Lord's deliverances. Check it out when you get a chance read Psalm 106 in its entirety, you will see that God continues to give His loved ones chance after chance to get it right. Here in verse 25 quoted above they murmured, and if you read on, you will see that they ended up in idolatry worshipping lifeless gods – all from the root cause of murmuring and not hearing God's voice and ending up in error. We must guard our hearts against complaining against God, against our brethren, against our family, against our situations and circumstances, and just murmuring in general.

2.12   Humble and Content
A safeguard from complaining and murmuring is to be found content. As in the following text:

> (1 Timothy 6:6) [And it is, indeed, a source of immense profit, for] godliness accompanied with contentment **(that**

contentment which is a sense of inward sufficiency) is great and abundant gain.

Godliness, which is a product of humility, has a cousin named contentment, which brings us great and abundant gain. Being called to greatness in the kingdom of God should produce humility, not pride. Having pride, or shall I say 'false pride' regarding yourself and what this greatness will produce, is actually failing the test for greatness and sends you around the mountain once again to break you into humility. You will get low and humble one way or another; either you will humble yourself, or you will get lifted up in pride and be brought down low. The choice is yours. We have the following scripture to show us how to operate in these trying times in which we currently live:

> (1 Peter 5:5b-11) …**Clothe (apron) yourselves, all of you, with humility [as the garb of a servant, so that its covering cannot possibly be stripped from you, with freedom from pride and arrogance]** toward one another. For God sets Himself against the proud (the insolent, the overbearing, the disdainful, the presumptuous, the boastful)—[and He opposes, frustrates, and defeats them], but gives grace (favor, blessing) to the humble. [6] Therefore humble yourselves [demote, lower yourselves in your own estimation] under the mighty hand of God, that in due time He may exalt you, [7] Casting the whole of your care [all your anxieties, all your worries, all your concerns, once and for all] on Him, for He cares for you affectionately and cares about you watchfully. [8] Be well balanced (temperate, sober of mind), be vigilant and cautious at all times; for that enemy of yours, the devil,

roams around like a lion roaring [in fierce hunger], seeking someone to seize upon and devour. ⁹ Withstand him; be firm in faith [against his onset—rooted, established, strong, immovable, and determined], knowing that the same (identical) sufferings are appointed to y—r brotherhood (the whole body of Christians) throughout the world. ¹⁰ And after you have suffered a little while, the God of all grace [Who imparts all blessing and favor], Who has called you to His [own] eternal glory in Christ Jesus, will Himself complete and make you what you ought to be, establish and ground you securely, and strengthen, and settle you. ¹¹ To Him be the dominion (power, authority, rule) forever and ever. Amen (so be it).

I could have stopped this quote at verse 5, but these other verses mean so much. Look at what the apron of humility will allow us to do! We can see ourselves in the proper estimation that God would have us see ourselves. This also empowers God to be able to exalt us in due time. It is when we are humble, aware of our lower state, that we can effectively cast our cares on Him and not carry those anxieties and burdens that attempt to rob us of joy and contentment in God. Humility helps us live balanced in our minds and see the enemy as the toothless roaring lion that he truly is. And I just love verse 10 because we see that these trials have a time – a little while – and in the process of enduring trials God is completing us! This is good news!

Know that God has made provisions for you to walk in humility according to Genesis 3:21 when He created skins and clothed Adam and Eve before putting them out of the garden. The humility is found in the type of shed blood, in the animal being killed here, which symbolizes none other than the Lord Jesus Christ to us today. We have to get a hold of the message of humility and walk in it because reading on in Genesis 3:24, we find that our access to the tree of Life is guarded and can only be accessed through Jesus, who is our example of humility. We must be found in Him.

To go a little deeper about what happened here in Genesis and why we must now speak to deception at its conception and not let it fester. God clothed them after they had eaten of the tree of knowledge of good and evil. He provided "skin" for them because prior to this point man had not recognized the "flesh" side of man because they were spirit…created in the image of God. Because they partook of the fruit of deception, sin and carnality entered the world – this was the point unhealthy pride entered the world.

Notice I said "unhealthy pride" because our pride should be based within God, not apart from Him. Our pride is in the fact that we are created in His image and likeness, it was the desire to be 'like God' that got Lucifer kicked out of heaven; and here in Genesis 3, he now came against God's creation in the form of a serpent and spoke this deception into existence. Not only did this birth sin due to the disobedience of man, but it began the age-old battle to do good apart *from* God that tries to disguise itself to look like it is *for* God. Just take a moment to ponder this section on being humble and content – reread it and allow God to reveal to you the enemies that are present to attack your ability to be humble and content, then go forward into the conclusion of this chapter ready to grow in this area.

2.13 Patience Train…
I would like to close out this chapter with what I have referred to as a "patience train" which is a chain or train link of texts that show how God works contentment and humility

into His children. Riding this train will help us be prepared for the assignment of *obedience* that the Lord has us on:

Luke 8:15

[15] But as for that [seed] in the good soil, these are [the people] who, hearing the Word, hold it fast in a just (noble, virtuous) and worthy heart, and steadily bring forth fruit with patience.

James 1:2-4

[2] Consider it wholly joyful, my brethren, whenever you are enveloped in or encounter trials of any sort or fall into various temptations. [3] Be assured and understand that the trial and proving of your faith bring out endurance and steadfastness and patience. [4] But let endurance and steadfastness and patience have full play and do a thorough work, so that you may be [people] perfectly and fully developed [with no defects], lacking in nothing.

Romans 5:3-5

[3] Moreover [let us also be full of joy now!] let us exult and triumph in our troubles and rejoice in our sufferings, knowing that pressure and affliction and hardship produce patient and unswerving endurance. [4] And endurance (fortitude) develops maturity of character (approved faith and tried integrity). And character [of this sort] produces [the habit of] joyful and confident hope of eternal salvation. [5] Such hope never disappoints or deludes or shames us, for God's love has been poured out in

2 Peter 1:5-9

⁵ For this very reason, adding your diligence [to the divine promises], employ every effort in exercising your faith to develop virtue (excellence, resolution, Christian energy), and in [exercising] virtue [develop] knowledge (intelligence), ⁶ And in [exercising] knowledge [develop] self-control, and in [exercising] self-control [develop] steadfastness (patience, endurance), and in [exercising] steadfastness [develop] godliness (piety), ⁷ And in [exercising] godliness [develop] brotherly affection, and in [exercising] brotherly affection [develop] Christian love. ⁸ For as these qualities are yours and increasingly abound in you, they will keep [you] from being idle or unfruitful unto the [full personal] knowledge of our Lord Jesus Christ (the Messiah, the Anointed One). ⁹ For whoever lacks these qualities is blind, [spiritually] shortsighted, seeing only what is near to him, and has become oblivious [to the fact] that he was cleansed from his old sins.

Romans 12:12

¹² Rejoice and exult in hope; be steadfast and patient in suffering and tribulation; be constant in prayer.

2 Timothy 2:24

²⁴ And the servant of the Lord must not be quarrelsome (fighting and contending). Instead, he must be kindly to everyone and mild-tempered [preserving the bond of peace]; he must be a skilled and suitable teacher, patient and forbearing and willing to suffer wrong.

Isaiah 48:10

[10] Behold, I have refined you, but not as silver; I have tried and chosen you in the furnace of affliction.

Hebrews 12:1

[1] Therefore then, since we are surrounded by so great a cloud of witnesses [who have borne testimony to the Truth], let us strip off and throw aside every encumbrance (unnecessary weight) and that sin which so readily (deftly and cleverly) clings to and entangles us, and let us run with patient endurance and steady and active persistence the appointed course of the race that is set before us.

CHAPTER 3 – FAILURE TO APPEAR

On Assignment— you know and recognize that you are on *assignment*. You have accepted it and acknowledged what is required of you. Yet you have failed to fulfill the *assignment*?! Lord— what do we do when we find ourselves here?

Prayer: I now pray for the people whose lives we are supposed to be on *assignment* in. Lord strengthen and encourage them by Your Spirit. People are waiting and wanting more of You. Lord continue to prick at the hearts of the people who are falling short of their *assignment*. Don't let them rest until they acknowledge their faults to You Lord. That You would be able to release the *assignment* to an obedient servant, or that they would rise up to the call. The reason some have not complied is because of distractions and the cares of this world. But that does not excuse them—it is only an excuse!

3.1 Resurrection Power

Sometimes in this "being *on assignment*" you may feel all alone and rejected – it could be because God is working some resurrection power in you. Yet look at what the Lord Jesus Christ endured on that cross. He looked around and was deserted by almost all of the people who once walked with Him. So we see that it is natural for this separation and aloneness to take place, it always occurs prior to a great resurrection in your life (or situation). Think it not strange when you find yourself all alone and it seems as if all who were supposed to be there have stepped away. You have to mount that cross individually – Oh but Joy comes in the morning, and just as sure as Christ was crucified, buried, and rose again on the third day, so will you rise out of this aloneness and rejection that you may experience in the process of answering the call to God. Notice that I said "in the process." You will have to live through some things and make it out on the other side whole. Will thou be made whole? The proof is in the putting, or shall we say in the standing— on God's word to see us through any and all situations and circumstances that come our way.

3.2 Questioning?

We should be cautious with our questionings as we are going through. I found two ways to ask a question when seeking the purpose or will of God in our life: 1) because we are hungry and want to know more details; or 2) to make a statement (legalism – wrong motives – as in Luke 10:25-37). When seeking God for clarity and direction in His plans and purposes it is okay to ask these first type questions. It is not unbelief, but weakness of faith, so asking the question and receiving the answer helps strengthen the faith system. But those second type questions won't receive the answer because there is no real hunger – and yet wrong motives – these are asked in doubt and unbelief, not really wanting the truth; and afraid to move out.

Here is an example of this concept with the young girl Mary. When the angel of the Lord explained her purpose, her destiny to her, she had a question "How can this be…?" This was the first type of question mentioned above, to get answers and further revelation. Her heart accepted it therefore she said: "Be it unto me as you have said." She gave heart-service, not just lip service and had actions following. It was after she began to walk it out that re-enforcement and strengthening took place with her visit to Elizabeth. During the process she strengthened someone else walking out a similar *obedience* test (See Luke 1). Another relevant point here is that Elizabeth and Zachariah were already in the midst of their trial as Mary was approached with her destiny trial. Proving that God is always orchestrating His plan even when we are un-aware, hence the need for us to pass these tests because other people are attached to our *obedience*.

For the past few years a theme scripture for me has been:

> (Job 42:3) [You said to me] Who is this that darkens and obscures counsel [by words] without knowledge? Therefore [I now see] I have [rashly] uttered what I did not understand, things too wonderful for me, which I did not know.

This text has caused me to make sure that my questions to God are for assistance illuminating my spiritual eyesight and understanding, not in doubt, unbelief, and distrust.

As I sat ready to embark on another major stage in this lifetime *assignment* that I am on, I wrote the following in my journal:

> Lord I thank You for life abundantly today. Although I still don't understand all that is happening to me, I do know that You are in

control and I will remain obedient to receive Your leading and guiding, direction and instruction.

We must remain humble enough to know and recognize that we don't have all the answers. Yet at the same time, we do not need all of the answers to be obedient to the "right now" instructions that we have or receive. As I went on and studied the entire Job chapter 42, which was the conclusion of a long *trial* that Job had experienced, I also noted another awesome principle that the Lord is relaying here:

> (Job 42:5) I had heard of You [only] by the hearing of the ear, but now my [spiritual] eye sees You.

So don't discount what you are going through as useless. These things come to help our spiritual eye to see God. The devil would love to make us think that these things happen because of something that we did, but he is a liar and there is no truth in him. If you go back to Job chapter 1, the enemy had to receive permission from God to do anything to Job. The purpose behind what the accuser was doing was trying to prove that Job didn't *really* love and reverently fear God. We need to make the devil a liar every time and hold on to what we believe in God. He is the Author and Finisher of our faith. He is the Lord God Jehovah Jireh that supplies our every need according to His riches in glory…and so on.

I noted that there were three friends that had weathered this trial with Job. However, they viewed things a little different than he did. Yet God was able to use even that to His glory.

> (Job 42:8) … and My servant Job shall pray for you, for I will accept [his prayer] that I deal not with you after your folly, in that you have not spoken of Me the thing that is right, as My servant Job has.

We are still to pray for others while it seems like we are still going through. God will receive it and restore double for your trouble. Something similar that I noticed with this text was Jesus in the garden, praying the "Not My will, but thine be done" prayer, He had brought 3 of His disciples with Him. Likewise, in Job's trial, there were 3 friends with him also. But notice this – Job had to go through the agonies in his flesh alone, even the 3 friends there couldn't ease what he had to go through; the same with Jesus; the same with you and I today. Just know that this too shall pass, and like Jesus, you will arise in the power and might of our Father.

> (1 Corinthians 15:57-58) But thanks be to God, Who gives us the victory [making us conquerors] through our Lord Jesus Christ. 58 Therefore, my beloved brethren, be firm (steadfast), immovable, always abounding in the work of the Lord [always being superior, excelling, doing more than enough in the service of the Lord], knowing and being continually aware that your labor in the Lord is not futile [it is never wasted or to no purpose].

A final word on getting in line with your *assignment*, although this above text is not talking specifically about our topic, we can pick up the principle of helping others labor in the Lord on purpose.

3.3   Mentoring – Divine connections

The first place to seek a mentor is the word of God. When I stumbled upon 1 John 2:27 as a teacher and mentor this scripture changed my life.

> (1 John 2:27, emphasis added) But as for you, the anointing (the sacred appointment, the unction) which you received from **Him abides [permanently] in you; [so] then you have no need that anyone should instruct you. But just as His anointing teaches you concerning everything and is true and is no falsehood**, so you must abide in (live in, never depart from) Him [being rooted in Him, knit to Him], just as [His anointing] has taught you [to do].

Don't get me wrong, it is a good thing to have a human agent that you can see and touch, and that is concerned about your well being; but in my case the Lord dealt with me alone first, then sent the mentors that basically confirmed and established the things I had been taught by the Holy Spirit my Teacher.

Another source of biblical mentorship is the book of Proverbs. To glean the nuggets of wisdom, godliness, and righteousness – as well to know clearly what is wicked, evil, and foolishness. I was advised at a young spiritual age to read through the book of Proverbs as a daily devotion; to allow the book of Proverbs to mentor me daily. In addition, I have found two daily devotionals that I have been reading for the last 7 years and will continue with the same two devotionals until the Lord says something different. One devotional is focused on prayer and time with God, and the other devotional is focused on the Holy Spirit and His workings in and through man. I have found that I have actually begun to live out these devotionals, not just read them.

The bible is full of all types of examples of mentoring that we can draw principles from: David and Jonathan; David and the 400 mighty men of war; Elijah and Elisha; Barnabas and Saul/Paul; Paul and Timothy, Silas, John Mark, Titus, and many others. But the best example is Jesus and His disciples.

I would like to talk a little about being called to mentor a person (or a project). I heard that mentoring is 85% relationship, thus mentoring someone will require you to develop a relationship of friendliness and trust. It is in developing this bond that you truly gain access into someone's life to help mold them into the person that God has designed them to be. Again, this level of personal mentoring will take time and transparency. If you are not ready to be open and honest with how you learned the word of God, or how God has dealt with you, you may not be ready to mentor someone just yet. It is not that you have to "tell your business," but that you tell how He brought you out and through some of the exact stuff that the mentee will be experiencing.

The Lord showed me early on that I don't have any business outside of His business because if it had not been for Him in my life I would not be here – so transparency is not an issue. The caution to use is to make sure that it is the Holy Spirit telling you to share, and not selfish motives, or zeal without knowledge. To make sure that you are healed, or working toward healing before you try to assist someone else in that area – because what would two people in wheelchairs look like trying to get up some stairs with no ramp? It would be difficult to assist. But if you were once in a wheelchair, have been healed from that ailment, and can now assist someone else make it up the stairs in a wheelchair with no ramp, then God is glorified because we are doing what Psalm 51:13 says about teaching transgressors God's ways. Personal mentoring will cut into your personal time, but the spiritual reward is worth it!

Personally I have had it both ways, to have a physical one-on-one mentor (not very much), and then to be mentored in the masses. Both ways work if you are truly seeking the Lord and whatever help He sends your way. There were a few women in my church in my younger spiritual years that mentored me and didn't even know it. I watched their perseverance, their devotion to the things of God, I could see an almost tangible anointing on them – even though everything was not roses, they never gave up, they continued to encourage others and do their part. Never once did we have one-on-one conversations, but they helped me so much. A comment that Mother Peridine (who was 99 years old at the time) said in a salutation was that she has read this same bible for over 70 something years, and every day she finds something new. That was just WOW to me! So I endeavor to have a similar testimony and don't grow tired in reading the bible over and over again, seeking out the new thing that God would show me this day. See, that was a mentoring nugget that I grabbed from a greeting! You can do this also.

I recently had a conversation with my Pastor about our mentoring relationship. I told him that our time of mentoring is on Sunday and Wednesday (the regular worship service with everyone else). This is why I can sit next to a person, hear the same message, yet receive so much more because this is our one-on-one time together – where I am receiving counsel and instructions from my mentor – like as if no one else is in the room. Now don't get me wrong, if I have an issue or a question or something I need explained more, I can call him and get his input, but at this level of maturity, I only call when I really need something – which makes him know that if I am calling, I must really need something, or for encouragement, or if the Lord is dealing with me to reach out to him.

Each person's mentoring relationships will vary, but lets try to not pull on another person more than we pull on God; and as mentors, lets make sure that we direct the people to God and show them how to access Him on their own as well as with our contact. As I told a young lady that has been in my life for over 11 years, "it is okay to call for help with the instructions, but I am not going to do the work for you. As in a math class, you must show your work, then I can assist you where you have gone wrong in problem solving." This is what our mentoring relationships should mature to over time.

Another concept to look at in mentoring is that of iron sharpens iron. Proverbs 27:17 says *Iron sharpens iron; so a man sharpens the countenance of his friend [to show rage or worthy purpose].* So both the person being mentored, and the person mentoring will receive a benefit. I have told several of the people that I mentor that it is not a burden, because God is not a user – He provides rewards because of our diligence to get to know the things of God. There have been times that I would assist a mentee with a concept or principle in the word, and then turn around in the very near future and need the very information that I assisted them with. Proving that God equips us as He sees fit, even if it is through helping someone else understand a concept or principle – this is active iron sharpening iron. Sometimes it is like deep calling to deep; the anointing in them pulling on the anointing in me (see Psalm 42:7) – or like Proverbs 20:5 *Counsel in the heart of man is like water in a deep well, but a man of understanding draws it out.* Just be a sounding board for them to work out their understanding of the word.

CHAPTER 4 – DEALING WITH THE HEART

4.1 Open before God

People often say, as an excuse for sin (for doing wrong or not doing what God has set forward) "God knows my heart..." and they are right, He does and that is why He is rebuking you for making excuses and worshipping (or serving) idols (i.e. your house, sports, the car, other events, your tired flesh, etc.). The following is a quote made by Tertullian, a 2nd century apologist, "Must you live? It is more important to be obedient to God than to be concerned with survival." He was saying that yes we have to live our daily lives, but *obedience* should be our main priority or goal.

> (Psalm 139:23-24) Search me [thoroughly], O God, and know my heart! Try me and know my thoughts! ^{24} And see if there is any wicked or hurtful way in me, and lead me in the way everlasting.

We have to give God complete access, and trust His all seeing and all knowing eye in the process. This psalm 139 is a good way to shine light on any hidden areas in our heart that we need to address. I love the Lord so much that He does not show everything to us at once, I don't think we could handle that. But as we come to Him daily, seeking Him daily, giving Him access into our heart daIly, He can and will unveil what needs to be seen. And as we find these areas, we can seek Him to clean our heart thoroughly.

The book of Psalms is man pouring out his soul (heart) to God. Why is it important for man to pour out his heart to God? That God may create in us a clean heart and a right spirit (Psalm 51:10). We want to be right with God, so it is important that we do our part. The entire 51st Psalm is a good place to begin with this cleaning and purging *portion* of allowing God to work into us the things that we need for life and godliness.

4.2 A clean heart
I would like to insert a restoration process according to Psalm 51 that I found to be similar to the time I re-finished my hardwood floors. I know it is a strange analogy but stick with me and you will see where I am coming from. Open your bible and follow along:

Step one – is to clean it. To sweep and gently wash away surface dirt.
>Psalm 51:1-2
>Hebrews 9:14

Step two – is to strip it. Remove the un-even and marred protector.
>Psalm 51:6-8
>Isaiah 1:25

Step three – is to sand it. Going even deeper than step two, going down to the original uncontaminated or exposed state.

Step four – is to stain it. Apply something that will make the natural wood be the desired color.
>Psalm 51:9
>Ephesians 1:11-14

Step five – to finish it.
>Psalm 51:10-12
>John 19:30

Step six – to seal it. Allow the Holy Spirit to have His way.
    Psalm 51:13-19
    2 Corinthians 1:21-22
    Ephesians 4:29-32

Step seven – bring beauty to it. Not part of Psalm 51, but a good conclusion to this restoration process.
    Psalm 61:1-3

Know that this is not a cute job, it was not fun or cute for me finishing my hardwood floors by myself because the people I asked for help were not available at the time I rented the equipment and needed to have things done, as this process relates to this analogy of restoring the heart, it is a personal job. I didn't think that I would be able to operate and handle that buffer or know how to apply the products for staining and sealing, but after much studying and the help of the Holy Spirit I completed those floors, and they looked good! So we to can do this process with our heart. You may feel abandoned by people, but this process is one in which you MUST do alone. Yet once the hard wood floor process is complete, the entire family and visitors can experience the beautiful change. As well, the completed process adds value to the property – the same with this heart process.

I would like to suggest a book that deals specifically with the heart that has helped me and many others. The book in reference is "Matters of The Heart: Stop Trying To Fix The Old, Let God Give You Something New" by Juanita Bynum (October 2002). The book is great and Prophetess Juanita shares an in depth message to the body of Christ that will "sho nuff" help you get your heart right. Yet again, I have been commissioned to share with you the actual things that I have learned in my personal studies as well.

4.3 Defining heart

As you read throughout the bible, you will find so many scriptures that refer to either the heart, the spirit, the mind or the soul. To me as a baby saint, or even in my more recent years, it used to really confuse me. So simply studying these definitions, coupled with attending church regularly and being exposed to them has helped me to know which was being referred to. Also, studying in the amplified bible helped me because the words are defined in parenthesis in text.

I wanted to do a simple word search to get some definitions to help understand what is meant by heart. So the following is what I found:

> **Heart**: personality, disposition, intellect; the emotional or moral as distinguished from the intellectual nature; one's innermost character, feelings or inclinations; the central or innermost part; center; the essential most vital part of something.

> **Spirit**: an animating or vital principle held to give life to physical organisms; a supernatural being or essence; temper or disposition of mind or outlook especially when vigorous or animated; a person having a character or disposition of a specified nature; a synonym is courage.

> **Mind**: recollection, memory; the element or complex of elements in an individual that feels, perceives, thinks, wills and especially reasons; intention, desire; opinion, view; disposition, mood.

> **Soul**: a person's total self; an active or essential part; a moving spirit; leader; the moral and emotional nature of human beings; the quality that arouses emotion and sentiment; fervor; a strong positive feeling (as of intense sensitivity and emotional fervor).
>
> (Proverbs 4:23 KJV) Keep thy heart with all diligence; for out of it are the issues of life.

The amplified bible actually states *"flow the springs of life."* So we can say that the springs are issues. Therefore, we must have godly things in our streams to heal the issues that people bring and need healing of. Our springs should first be health and healing to us, and the overflow be available to bring help to others. The next verse is the clincher to what we are to instruct the people about:

> (Proverbs 4:24) Put away from you false and dishonest speech, and willful and contrary talk put far from you.

We ourselves have to make conscious changes in our attitude and vocabulary. An example of willful and contrary talk is to doubt what you heard God say in regards to you and your *assignment*. Don't get caught up in this, simply put, stop the foolish questionings once you have what the word says. Speak the word!

> (Psalm 17:3 KJV) Thou has proved my heart; thou hast visited me in the night; thou has tried me, and shalt find nothing; I am purposed that my mouth shall not transgress.

Here is an example of an inside job (or work) of God. The latter part of this scripture says, "I am purposed that my mouth shall not transgress". We have to put our mouth under subjection to purpose it not to transgress. I looked up the word transgress in the regular dictionary and found this "to go beyond or over (a limit or boundary); to act in violation of (a law, commandment, etc.)". Then I took it a step further to the Vine's Complete Expository Dictionary and one of the definitions there was "to rebel; the state of rebellion in which there is no end of the rebellion in view." So we must purpose our mouth to not speak of rebellion. You may ask how do I stop my mouth? Glad you asked. This refers back to controlling what you are thinking on. You bring your mouth into subjection in your thought life, think on godly things, not rebellious things. What you think on most, you will act out.

> (Psalm 19:13-14) Keep back Your servant also from presumptuous sins; let them not have dominion over me! Then shall I be blameless, and I shall be innocent and clear of great transgression. [14] Let the words of my mouth and the meditation of my heart be acceptable in Your sight, O Lord, my [firm, impenetrable] Rock and my Redeemer.
>
> (Jeremiah 17:10) I, the Lord, search the mind, I try the heart, even to give every man according to his ways, according to the fruit of his doings.

We can take this searching of the mind a step further. When the Lord shows you yourself, as you asked Him to, and as He told you He would do, we must DO what the Lord shows us to do. We will begin to see things deep down and buried within our heart. Things like doubt, unforgiveness, etc. We must not dwell on what He shows us, we must continue to seek and prepare for what He has called us to do. The purpose for Him showing us these things is for us to ask Him to help us out (see Psalm 139:23-24). We have His spirit living within us that is the Helper to help us with all things.

> (Proverbs 4:20-23 KVJ) My son, attend to my words; incline thine ear unto my sayings. Let them not depart from thine eyes; keep them in the midst of thine heart. For they are life unto those that find them, and health to all their flesh.

The amplified bible says, "let them not depart from your SIGHT." This coupled with "keep them in the center of your HEART" is talking about seeing with your heart. We are definitely dealing with the heart issues. The scripture goes on to let us know that when we do these things, we will find life, and then more than just life, we will find health to ALL our flesh. I took this personally and noted that my children are flesh from within my being, so this word that I hold in my heart is health to even their flesh. It is my job to teach this principle to them so that they walk in the divine health promised.

I am not just blurting out a lot of rules. We must be careful that our goal is to get to know God more and more personally. Actually developing a relationship with Him that goes two ways. We must be careful because rules without relationship lead to rebellion. Then we end up in a vicious cycle of quoting scriptures without the relationship that is required to bring them to past.

4.4 Jesus and your heart

When I queried on biblegateway.com for the word "heart" in the gospels in the amplified bible I found over 90 mentions of heart. This should give us an indication that Jesus is concerned with our heart. My Pastor brought out a good point that Jesus is so concerned with our heart (as defined earlier – our attitude) that He began His first public sermon in Matthew 5 talking about the issues of the heart with the beatitudes.

> (Matthew 5:8) Blessed (happy, enviably fortunate, and spiritually prosperous— possessing the happiness produced by the experience of God's favor and especially conditioned by the revelation of His grace, regardless of their outward conditions) are the pure in heart, for they shall see God!

I read through those 90 mentions and saw a theme to caution those who are *On Assignment* of: some people hardened their hearts and would not change or repent.

> (Matthew 11:20) Then He began to censure and reproach the cities in which most of His mighty works had been performed, because they did not repent [and their hearts were not changed].

I will touch on repentance toward the end of this chapter but know that Jesus reads people's heart and He reproved heart actions, or assisted in strengthening the heart.

> (Mark 6:50) For they all saw Him and were agitated (troubled and filled with fear and dread). But immediately He talked with them and said, Take heart! I AM! Stop being alarmed and afraid.

> (Ezekiel 36:26-27) A new heart will I give you and a new spirit will I put within you, and I will take away the stony heart out of your flesh and give you a heart of flesh. And I will put my Spirit within you and cause you to walk in My statutes, and you shall heed My ordinances and do them

The following in is an excerpt from Vine's Expository:

> The "heart" stands for the inner being of man, the man himself. As such, it is the fountain of all he does (Proverbs 4:4). All his thoughts, desires, words, and actions flow from deep within him. Yet a man cannot understand his own "heart" (Jeremiah 17.9). As a man goes on in his own way, his "heart" becomes harder and harder. But God will circumcise (cut away the uncleanness of) the "heart" of His people, so that they will love and obey Him with their whole being (Deuteronomy 30:6).

Isn't this some awesome news! That although we cannot understand our heart, we know that God will lead us in getting the things out of our inner being that will cause us damage. We must be obedient to the Lord's leading to not end up with a hardened, rebellious heart.

Joy comes in the morning. The morning is actually when we wake up, or are woken up to the Truth. That Truth is that our joy is in the Lord. Also, we bring the joy to others when we are obedient and do what God instructs us to do. It doesn't have to be in the physical morning, the morning is when ever the Light is recognized or realized shining in our situation (circumstances).

Lord, open their eyes from the blindness that is going on. Like the blind man at the gate Beautiful, Lord heal them of their blindness, cause them to take off the blind man's clothes and come into the temple worshipping and praising You O God (as in John 9).

4.5 Holiness – the worshipper's heart
The heart of a true worshipper should be holiness. Holiness is a matter of the heart. Let's examine 2 familiar texts that are used for worship and see the heart issues (Genesis 22 and John 4). First, in Genesis 22 Abraham received some specific instructions as God was testing his heart for idolatry and to see if he would withhold anything from God.

> (Genesis 22:3) So Abraham rose early in the morning, saddled his donkey, and took two of his young men with him and his son Isaac; and he split the wood for the burnt offering, and then began the trip to the place of which God had told him.

Again, we see that these heart issues are something that must be handled personally. Notice that Abraham had people with him that were probably more able-bodied than he, but we see that **he** prepared the wood for this sacrifice of a burnt offering. The burnt offering, according to Leviticus 1 was to be a "sweet and satisfying odor to the Lord." The wood has many symbols in scripture and as I was searching for which symbol applies here, I found the following *"wood represents Christian activities, which look big, but have little value in God's sight...and do not stand the searching judgment of God"* – so we are being tested to make sure that our service is unto the Lord, not man or anything else that will not stand the judgment of God.

> (Genesis 22:5) And Abraham said to his servants, Settle down and stay here with the donkey, and I and the young man will go yonder and worship and come again to you.

Some of our worship *assignments* will not make any logical sense – but we don't take our cues from logic, but the Spirit of God. Here in this text (verse 1) Abraham was being tested and proved by God (not man), he had been given specific yet vague instructions (verse 2), and he arose early in the morning (verse 3) to follow out the instructions. In an immature state, these instructions could have been botched.

Another personal aspect or example to note about a burnt offering and sacrifice to the Lord of worship is seen by looking at King David (see 1 Chronicles 21 and 2 Samuel 24, both are the same story). His heart had just been tested by God (in verse 1), and he didn't do too well on the test, because of His failure 70,000 of his men were killed in one day! Do you see the importance of getting stuff right, your actions not only affect you, but others. As he went through the heart process, he received instructions to build an altar to the Lord on a specific threshing floor (location). The owner of the threshing floor offered to give King David the materials and the threshing floor, but David replied (in verse 24 of both texts, ironic huh…) that *I will not offer burnt offerings to the Lord my God of that which costs me nothing… I will not take what is yours for the Lord, nor offer burnt offerings which cost me nothing.* This is a personal process.

4.6   *In spirit and truth*

John 4 is the second text in reference; Jesus and the Samaritan woman. She had walls up and put up a front before Jesus. Jesus found the issue in her heart that she needed to lay on the altar – her seeking in man what only God can give (see verse 16-18).

> (John 4:22-24) You [Samaritans] do not know what you are worshiping [you worship what you do not comprehend]. We do know what we are worshiping [we worship what we have knowledge of and understand], for [after all] salvation comes from [among] the Jews. [23] A time will come, however, indeed it is already here, when the true (genuine) worshipers will worship the Father in spirit and in truth (reality); for the Father is seeking just such people as these as His worshipers. [24] God is a Spirit (a spiritual Being) and those who worship Him must worship Him in spirit and in truth (reality).

Spirit and truth. Having truth brings righteousness. It is the truth of the gospel of Jesus Christ and the kingdom of God that brings salvation and the imputed righteousness of Jesus Christ the Messiah. Another offspring of the truth is humility as discussed earlier in chapter 2.

The process 86ettingg a clean heart is a daily, continual process. Some things will be instantaneous, but others will take a while to be dealt with. It is like brushing your teeth, you don't just do that one time, it is a daily thing. So examine your own heart daily to make sure there is no "plaque" build up or issues lying dormant in your heart.

Back to John 4

> (John 4:28-29 – emphasis added) Then the woman **left her water jar and went away** to the town. And **she began telling the people,** ²⁹ Come, see a Man Who has told me everything that I ever did! Can this be [is not this] the Christ? [Must not this be the Messiah, the Anointed One?]

She left the drama behind – those issues that were in her heart. She went and evangelized in her town. Yet know that this will bring on another level of accountability with people watching you walk the walk you talk.

Having our heart right before God is an issue of trust. Do you truly trust God and the truth to produce in you the clean heart; the purged heart; the right heart; that will empower you to walk in spirit and truth; to be presented as the righteousness of God in Christ? It is about trust, and engaging the tools that God has provided. He provides the tools, which are the word of God and Jesus Christ as our example, but He will not do the work for you. You must walk it out. Abraham had to follow the instructions, the Samaritan woman believed, left her water jar, and went and declared what she had heard. This all begins in the heart, with what we believe in our heart. This is why Proverbs 4:23 says to *guard your heart for out of it flow the issues of life.*

4.7 *Guard your heart*

> (Jeremiah 17:9) The heart is deceitful above all things, and it is exceedingly perverse and corrupt and severely, mortally sick! Who can

> know it [perceive, understand, be acquainted with his own heart and mind]?

This is why we must guard our heart and rely on the Holy Spirit to assist in the regular examination of our heart. We are prone to being deceived and deceiving others if we remain with an un-checked and un-examined heart.

> (Romans 12:1-2, emphasis added) I appeal to **you** therefore, brethren, and beg of **you** in view of [all] the mercies of God, to make a decisive dedication of **your** bodies [presenting all **your** members and faculties] as a living sacrifice, holy (devoted, consecrated) and well pleasing to God, which is **your** reasonable (rational, intelligent) service and spiritual worship. ² **Do not be conformed** to this world (this age), [fashioned after and adapted to its external, superficial customs], **but be transformed** (changed) by the [entire] renewal of **your** mind [by its new ideals and its new attitude], so that **you** may prove [for **yourselves**] what is the good and acceptable and perfect will of God, even the thing which is good and acceptable and perfect [in His sight for **you**].

Notice how many times this Romans 12:1-2 has the phrase "**you**" – emphasizing that **you** must put forth some effort in the process. This is first an issue of the heart – you have to allow your spirit to lead, and renew your mind to make it possible to present your body (your Isaac) on the altar.

We have our part, and God has His part. He sits as the Refiner of our hearts:

> (Malachi 3:2-3) But who can endure the day of His coming? And who can stand when He appears? For He is like a refiner's fire and like fullers' soap; ³ He will sit as a refiner and purifier of silver, and He will purify the priests, the sons of Levi, and refine them like gold and silver, that they may offer to the Lord offerings in righteousness.

> (Zechariah 13:9) And I will bring the third part through the fire, and will refine them as silver is refined and will test them as gold is tested. They will call on My name, and I will hear and answer them. I will say, It is My people; and they will say, The Lord is my God.

4.8 Heart confession

I would like to close this chapter with a heart confession according to scripture:

Psalm 51:2-3, 10 Wash me thoroughly [and repeatedly] from my iniquity and guilt and cleanse me and make me wholly pure from my sin! For I am conscious of my transgressions and I acknowledge them; my sin is ever before me...Create in me a clean heart, O God, and renew a right, persevering, and steadfast spirit within me.

Psalm 51:16-19 MSG $^{16\text{-}17}$ Going through the motions doesn't please you, a flawless performance is nothing to you. I learned God-worship when my pride was shattered. Heart-shattered lives ready for love don't for a moment escape God's notice. [18-19] Make Zion the place you delight in, repair Jerusalem's broken-down walls. Then you'll get real worship from us, acts of worship small and large, including all the bulls they can heave onto your altar!

Psalm 139: 23-24 Search me [thoroughly], O God, and know my heart! Try me and know my thoughts! And see if there is any wicked or hurtful way in me, and lead me in the way everlasting.

Romans 12:2 Do not be conformed to this world (this age), [fashioned after and adapted to its external, superficial customs], but be transformed (changed) by the [entire] renewal of your mind [by its new ideals and its new attitude], so that you may prove [for yourselves] what is the good and acceptable and perfect will of God, even the thing which is good and acceptable and perfect [in His sight for you].

Psalm 19:13-14 Keep back Your servant also from presumptuous sins; let them not have dominion over me! Then shall I be blameless, and I shall be innocent and clear of great transgression. Let the words of my mouth and the meditation of my heart be acceptable in Your sight, O Lord, my [firm, impenetrable] Rock and my Redeemer.

CHAPTER 5 – NOT OF THIS WORLD

5.1 The world hates you

> (John 15:19 NIV) If you belonged to the world, it would love you as its own. As it is, you do not belong to the world, but I have chosen you out of the world. That is why the world hates you.

Not of this world. That is more than just a thought. The more and more I study and get to know God personally through the Lord Jesus Christ in the written word, the more I see that I am definitely not of this world. It used to baffle me when I would be ridiculed for attending church a lot (more than the average person), and then one day I stumbled upon this scripture. These were actually the words of Jesus telling His disciples that they would be hated because He was hated. This alleviated a lot of pressure off of me and let me know that as long as I am pleasing God, it is not up to man, or better yet, the things of this world, to bring me peace. For only the Lord can bring that. In this chapter I plan to share a few examples of "Not of This World" to help those of us *On Assignment* know when to not take it personal because you are "Not of This World".

In the gospels of Matthew and Mark, Jesus said that He would make them fishers of men. A slang term that I used to use was "off the hook". Yes, man is literally off the hook without Jesus, and on the road to a flesh ruled (carnal) life. As fishermen, we are to get them hooked on Jesus and receive that eternal life. And just as fish cannot live outside of their natural environment, so born again believers need to be in an environment of Christ (the things of God) to survive.

Looking at some of the things of this world, I have noticed that one of the enemy's tools (tactics) has been deceit – like with woman in the garden, he deceived her by mixing doubt with the instructions. He will try to condemn us and cause us to feel as if we don't fit in, or that we have lost our mind. Well, guess what? You DON'T fit in, and you should have lost your mind and received the mind of Christ. You don't fit in because you are an alien, and you are speaking God's language which man in and of himself cannot and will not receive.

5.2   *Strangers and aliens*

> (Hebrews 11:13 NIV) All these people were still living by faith when they died. They did not receive the things promised; they only saw them and welcomed them from a distance. And they admitted that they were **aliens and strangers** on earth.

> (2 Peter 2:11) Dear friends, I urge you, as **aliens and strangers** on earth, to abstain from sinful desires which war against your soul

Even though we are often times unsure, we must be obedient to what the Spirit of the Lord has called us to do or say because He is in control. Yet there are times that our stubbornness, slothfulness, or rebelliousness causes great delays. We must stop this from within at the onset.

God is waiting, just like Jesus waited when He was called to come see about Lazarus. He knew that there was a need for His presence there. Just as He knows that we have a need. It seems as if He has forgotten, doesn't care, or just has lost

His mind. But He is waiting for us to lay there and be dead. What do dead people do? Nothing! We need to stop trying to fix stuff, trying to add perfume (a I) to cover up the stench. We need to lay there dead to self:

> Dead to self – understanding
> Dead to self – knowledge
> Dead to self – trying to fix and do Jesus' work

Die to self and rest in the Lord Jesus Christ. That is when you will hear that call from Jesus for Lazarus to come forward. He will call you by name to come forward. When we get in that state of rest in Him, and we are squeezed by pressures and circumstances, all that should come out of us is the goodness of God, knowing that our steps are ordered by the Lord. We can do this by resting in Him as He has said, "come unto Me…and I will give you rest." This rest is the same rest referred to here:

> (Hebrews 4:10) For he who has once entered [God's] rest also has ceased from [the weariness and pain] of human labors, just as God rested from those labors peculiarly His own

5.3 Do You Really KNOW Him?

> (Matthew 7:23 NIV) Then I will tell them plainly, 'I never **knew** you. Away from me, you evildoers!'

You may have begun to be acquainted with Him, you may have flirted with Him, but you can NOT be intimate with

God and idols. That is adultery; a form of attempted polygamy; and God is not having that! We cannot walk into a deeper relationship with God and continue to do the idolatrous things that we once did. The latter part of this text in the King James Version, the phrase "evildoers" is replaced as "ye that work iniquity". I researched the word iniquity and came up with this:

> Iniquity: gross injustice; wickedness a wicked act; or sin.

Also, in researching "iniquity" in the Vine's Expository Dictionary, I found the following interesting facts:

> Its usual rendering in the New Testament means unrighteousness. A condition of not being right, whether with God, according to the standard of what man knows to be right by his conscience. Denotes lawlessness, transgression, unrighteousness.

So basically, the point that I am trying to make here is that we must walk in the righteousness that we have in Christ Jesus and not be led astray with the evil thoughts and acts that seem to be commonplace in the society around us.

As an alien and being "Not of This World" we must learn to feed on the proper diet. I'm not talking about natural food. Although it is important to eat properly and exercise our body, for it is the temple of the living God. But I am talking about spiritual food. Just as in the natural we have what is called metabolism, the less you need to consume, or the more you need to exercise to burn the food that you consume. We need to feed our spirit man just like our natural man, and some of us need to watch what we are eating as well as exercise to be fit both naturally and spiritually.

> (Isaiah 54:17 KJV) No weapon that is formed against thee shall prosper; and every tongue that shall rise against thee in judgment thou shalt condemn. This is the heritage of the servants of the LORD, and their righteousness is of me, saith the LORD.

No weapon shall prosper against you; therefore you should have a junkyard in your honor of all the weapons that have formed, but not prospered. Instead, some people have made the enemy rich because he has been prospering with his weapons on them. STOP! You have the authority to tell the devil no. It is you that has to stand up as the righteousness of God in Christ Jesus and apply this to your situation; this text says your righteousness is of Me! I also want you to understand that these things will arise – this text tells us that they will come. But you hold on to what He said next – it SHALL NOT PROSPER! No way! Cast it out in the name of Jesus. You can hook the Old Testament up with the New Testament and say: "Who shall separate me from the Love of God?"

> (Romans 8:38-39) For I am persuaded beyond doubt (am sure) that neither death nor life, nor angels nor principalities, nor things impending and threatening nor things to come, nor powers, [39] Nor height nor depth, nor anything else in all creation will be able to separate us from the love of God which is in Christ Jesus our Lord.

Here is a future study for me to suggest to those who want to really do some damage to the kingdom of darkness: look in Esther chapter 8 and see the genocide that the enemy set up for the Jewish people. See how the king went back and reversed that to cause anyone that would rise up against the

Jewish people to be killed an even worse death. Compare that to what we now have in our rights as children of God, our sonship and inheritance with our Brother Jesus. We cannot stand up to our enemy (satan) with our own authority – but with God's word. And the spoil belongs to the kingdom of God.

> (Esther 8:11) In it the king granted the Jews who were in every city to gather and defend their lives; to destroy, to slay, and to wipe out any armed force that might attack them, their little ones, and women; and to take the enemies' goods for spoil.

5.4   Get the "L" out
I would like to conclude this chapter with a quote from one of my pastors. The title of his message was "Get the 'L' out". He was referring to taking the 'L' out of the W-O-R-L-D and having only the W-O-R-D left. This is a cute way of looking at why we must get in the word of God. Study it regularly to get the 'L' out of us, to get the world out. Also, some people say there is not fame in studying the word of God and having a relationship with God. When you take the 'L' out of the world, and place it into this word FAME, you now have FLAME. I desire to be a burning flame for the Lord, continually fueled by the Holy Spirit. When we get the 'L' in the proper prospective is when we realize that the 'L' stands for LOVE. Not of this world but of being a servant, an alien *on assignment* in a foreign land.

On Assignment

CHAPTER 6 – THE GREAT FALL

6.1 Temptation
After being saved for 15 years, actually serving the Lord for 8 years, spirit filled, sold out to the cause of Christ (aware of my rights as the righteousness of God in Christ), I found myself in a place that I thought I would never be. In sin! I made a God decision, yet I crossed over into the flesh and messed up majorly. Some of the solitude that we experience is the Lord's doing; for His purpose. We have to be careful to not begin in the spirit and end in the flesh. The devil is a liar and will not get the glory that is due to God.

The enemy tried to talk me into giving up on my relationship with God. He began to show me pictures of people laughing and mocking at me and saying "I thought she was saved, Ms. Preacher Lady." For one split second it was too much to fathom, so out of habit I cried out to God for help and His response to me was, "Who are you allowing to talk to you? Does that sound like something I'd say? Run him out now! Like woman should have done in the garden! Don't lose your position with Me by listening to him!" So the following chapter is the process of what I went through to maintain fellowship, and continue diligently serving God after a great fall.

There are several types of sin that bear consequences. Most people just think of sexual sin, but the list is far greater than that. Here is a brief list of possibilities:

- What about the person that entered a marriage relationship against the will of God, and against the suggestions of their family or church members. Consequences.
- Or the person that moved to a new city, without the leading of God, and now everything is blowing up in your face and nothing seems to be working right. Consequences.
- Then there is the person that left their job for another job with more pay (again, without consulting God) and now this new job lays you off and you are thrown into a financial down spiral. Consequences.
- You needed a new vehicle because the one you had kept breaking down. So you went and bought that brand new car. Months later you are seriously struggling to maintain the gas, insurance, and payment. Then you realize that you never consulted God. Consequences.
- Then there are those of us who thought we were believing God for provision, but were really in pride when the Lord told us who to consult for assistance. Now things are out of control. Consequences.
- Maybe you were single, sold out and living for the Lord, celibate and chaste for several years. Then one night of weakness to the flesh lands you with a deadly disease, or pregnant. Consequences.

6.2   Get back up, run back in

Missing the mark – yet getting up, repenting and continuing to press toward the mark. As long as you are in this earth suit, you are in a race. It isn't over until you change suits, so make the most of it. Stay in the word – keep it ever before you.

We are in a race, and a hit hurdle will not stop the race. Yes, hitting the hurdle hurts, and it may slow down your finish time, but a good runner will run on and complete the race. I ran track in high school and I asked my coach why we had to keep going after a hit hurdle since we know we probably won't win the race? His response was "it is a principle that we finish what we start, no matter what we place in the race" – not to mention some people have won the event in spite of a hit hurdle. Also, hit hurdles teach us how to run better in the future making sure that we do not hit anymore hurdles, thus avoiding more pain than necessary. The same is true in the spirit realm of running a race.

They that hunger and thirst. If you are truly hungering and thirsting, a bad decision should not stop you. You won't be so quick to jump ship just because you made a bad decision (or maybe a few bad decisions). As soon as you come to yourself (and don't wait until you end up in the pig pen), turn quickly, AS SOON AS POSSIBLE, and repent (Luke 15 about the prodigal son).

> (1 John 1:9) If we confess our sins, he is faithful and just to forgive us our sins, and to cleanse us from all unrighteousness.

With your whole heart turn. He is faithful and just to cover you with His grace and mercy. As Dad Hagin says, "This is just another opportunity to prove that God's word works." So learn from it, grow, and become what you need to be through this trial.

Don't get caught up into religious acts trying to restore your position in Christ. It is by faith, your forgiveness is there, accept it.

Yet this message is not a lesson to live crazy. God will not be mocked, don't keep falling to the same issue. You are playing and you need to quit. You are only fooling yourself, not God, you may need to take it a step further and ask for deliverance. For God looks upon your heart and that is where He judges. So you should be ever judging yourself and get your heart right before God. Notice I said before **God**, not man. If God be for me, who can be against me. So purpose to be right before Him and things will eventually work for your good because you will have all of heaven backing you. Don't stay stuck on stupid – decide to repent, turn completely away from drama outside of God's will.

Looking at the first drama with mankind in the Garden of Eden; the drama was birthed from disobedience – they disobeyed the instructions, and the consequence was that sin brought separation from the original intent of mankind. Adam and Eve were not just put out without provisions; God covered them and set up redemption for them:

> (Genesis 3:21) For Adam also and for his wife the Lord God made long coats (tunics) of skins and clothed them.

We usually read right over this verse without realizing that an animal had to die in order to make this tunic (coat). Blood had to be shed to lay the way for the plan of redemption that God spoke of in Genesis 3 verse 15. The nakedness of man that once was not an issue (because his heart was right before God, but then sin caused a breech), now had to be covered, and someone would lose their life – although this was not a human being, it was still something that God created. This text also reminds me of the obedience test that Abraham went through with Isaac, the Lord provided there, and this is where we find the covenant name Jehovah Jireh the Lord that Provides (in Genesis 22); but notice here, an animal was sacrificed to complete this test. Both tests were of the heart, God examining and protecting the heart, yet it had outward symbols.

This was all symbolic of the Lord Jesus Christ, as John the Baptist said: "behold the Lamb that takes away the sin of the world." It is through the Lord Jesus Christ clothing us with His righteousness, His mind and thoughts, all of His "IS"-ness – that empowers us to live on today in spite of all that is going on around us, and in spite of the constant temptations. We are alive today and redemption is for us in Jesus Christ! Receive it; and pursue to maintain it.

> (Philippians 2:12) Therefore, my dear ones, as you have always obeyed [my suggestions], so now, not only [with the enthusiasm you

would show] in my presence but much more because I am absent, work out (cultivate, carry out to the goal, and fully complete) your own salvation with reverence and awe and trembling (self-distrust, with serious caution, tenderness of conscience, watchfulness against temptation, timidly shrinking from whatever might offend God and discredit the name of Christ).

This scripture was written to a group of people who knew that they didn't have to work for salvation, it was already theirs (and works didn't get it for them). Therefore, this is stating that salvation is based upon believing Jesus in your heart – is talking about living a life of salvation – and talking about what you should do since your ARE saved. You should live with respect and awe to God. Live a lifestyle knowing that you have salvation and your desire is to please God. Even when you miss it, confess it immediately. The sin is not pleasing to God, and you cannot have fellowship and communion with Him with sin in your life, so deal with it as soon as it occurs, or better yet, just refrain from it all together.

The devil is a liar! So don't listen to his lies. Don't dread people, fear God only. It is God who is your Provider, your All in all. Please Him and the other people can go to God with their issues. Just know that the devil will try to paint a grim picture, he is a liar. The devil's goal is to bring condemnation, but our Father's goal is to bring conviction that leads to repentance.

The Holy Spirit within us acts as our agent of conviction; of change. He lives within us to stop us from getting into trouble. If we press right pass Him and get into trouble anyway, He is still there drawing us to repent and get it right before God. Don't mistake His tug as condemnation. Romans 8:1 says: *For there is therefore no condemnation to them who are in Christ Jesus.*

> (John 5:24) I assure you, most solemnly I tell you, the person whose ears are open to My words [who listens to My message] and believes and trusts in and clings to and relies on Him Who sent Me has (possesses now) eternal life. And he does not come into judgment [does not incur sentence of judgment, will not come under condemnation], but he has already passed over out of death into life.

> (John 5:24 KJV) Verily, verily, I say unto you, He that heareth my word, and believeth on him that sent me, hath everlasting life, and shall not come into condemnation; but is passed from death unto life.

My dear friend, now is NOT the time to run *from* the church, *from* the bible, or *from* fellowship with the saints. NO! That is what the devil wants you to do so that he can continue to walk on you, play with you, keep you outside of God's will, and devour you. NO – run into the multitude of safety! Yes, it may seem like Everyone is picking on you, and they are catering their message to your issue (but they aren't, that is the conviction we talked about earlier), be strong in the Lord and continue to choose to not quit. Disappoint the devil, not God! Let the devil down, don't do what he is telling and yelling for you to do. He is the thief that kills, steals and destroys. His tauntings will always be about these 3 things: killing, stealing, and destroying. BUT GOD! God's leading will always be about life, love and abundance. The devil's suggestions subtract and reduce you; while God's leading will restore you and build you up.

Yes, there are some consequences that we will have to face. But life is not over – God gives His grace and mercy to live through the consequences of disobedience. So you may have to go into that international ministry that you have been preparing for with a child. Or you may have to repair your credit first. Know this, your life is not over, just added on to. Yet you have God's favor still upon your life to succeed in this also. And yes, things may be delayed a little because of your choices, but delay is not denial. Also know this, this delay is not *from* God, but from our own actions and decisions.

But my loved ones, Romans 8:28 tells us that ALL things work together for the good of them that love the Lord and are called according to His purpose.

> (Romans 8:26-28 KJV emphasis added) Likewise the Spirit also helpeth our infirmities: for we know not what we should pray for as we ought: but the Spirit itself maketh intercession for us with groanings which cannot be uttered. And he that searcheth the hearts knoweth what is the mind of the Spirit, because he maketh intercession for the saints according to the will of God. And we know that **ALL**

THINGS work together for good to them that love God, to them who are the called according to his purpose.

6.3   Talking About ALL Things...

Look at Joseph in the pit. Although he ended up there not by his own choice. He was in a pit, a dark place, alone, isolated, yet he kept a small flicker of hope. The places that he ended up (the pit, the prison, and the palace) did not stop him from holding on to his dream. So why would we allow our manmade pits and prisons to squash our dreams? NO – the time is now, even though you may have messed up on your own. God's favor doesn't have to depart from you if you will but humble yourself. Repent. Follow hard after the Lord.

> (2 Chronicles 7:14) If my people, which are called by my name, shall humble themselves, and pray, and seek my face, and turn from their wicked ways; then will I hear from heaven, and will forgive their sin, and will heal their land.

Don't lose fellowship and go out wandering in a wilderness longer than you must. We will all have wilderness events in life. In order to survive these events we must rely on God for our daily sustenance. You can't get fed if you are hiding from Him. Don't go off trying to make provisions for yourself. You know that God is a greater provider than we could ever be. NOTE: the devil is not a provider; he is a deceiver. Why would he provide for you to live? His mission is to kill, steal and destroy, not give life. DON'T LISTEN TO HIM!

> (Matthew 6:33) But seek (aim at and strive after) first of all His kingdom and His righteousness (His way of doing and being right), and then all these things taken together will be given you besides.

Be kingdom minded, stay kingdom minded. Don't allow a bad decision to cloud and blur your vision of the kingdom. The circumstances have changed, but the kingdom of God has not. Seek after this kingdom. Again, it is a heart posture. There is the kingdom of God in each of us. Thy kingdom come, we can say, "Come alive in me today."

Don't turn your back on all the teaching and instruction that you have received prior to your fall, it still works. Get up, shake it off, and apply that word to this situation. Pull that word up out of your internal message bank and apply it today. Don't give up on it, apply it. And it may take more than one application to stick; yet be diligent about allowing the word to work in you. It will work if you work it.

6.4 Better or bitter?

> (Ephesians 4:31) Let all **bitterness** and indignation and wrath (passion, rage, bad temper) and resentment (anger, animosity) and quarreling (brawling, clamor, contention) and slander (evil-speaking, abusive or blasphemous language) be

banished from you, with all malice (spite, ill will, or baseness of any kind)

(Hebrews 12:15) Exercise foresight and be on the watch to look [after one another], to see that no one falls back from and fails to secure God's grace (His unmerited favor and spiritual blessing), in order that no root of resentment (rancor, **bitterness**, or hatred) shoots forth and causes trouble and **bitter** torment, and the many become contaminated and defiled by it—

Let this trial make you *bEtter* and not *bItter*.

Better = E = eternally minded.

Bitter = I = selfishly minded.

When we allow the situations and circumstances of life to make us bitter, this is actually a selfish thing – only thinking about "I" (me and mine). This will cause you to make even more bad decisions and alienate you further from God. But when we choose to allow these same situations and circumstances to make us better, we are headed in the right direction to reap eternal benefits.

You get more bees with honey (*bEtter*) than with vinegar (*bItter*). We do influence those that are around watching us go through trials. Do you want to influence them the *bEtter* way, or the *bItter* way? Remember, souls are what we are after, you may be the only bible people are reading, or the only witness for the Lord Jesus Christ in someone's life. They are watching how we go through our trials and circumstances. So we must be aware of how we go through.

I just wanted to take a moment here at the conclusion of this chapter to note that I almost did not go forward with this chapter because Bishop TD Jakes has written an excellent book titled "Help, I've Fallen And I Can't Get Up". However, the Lord reminded me that He had allowed me to write over ¾ of this chapter before I came upon this book. Also, that my story is not the same as Bishop's, so my input must go forward. Yet I earnestly encourage you to get a hold of this book by Bishop Jakes and apply it as well.

CHAPTER 7 – DISTRACTIONS

Distractions. Lets define the word to assure that we are all thinking about the same thing. The American Heritage dictionary defines 'distract' as: to turn aide; divert; to stir up or confuse with conflicting emotions or motives; puzzle. It also defines 'divert' as: deviate; to turn from one course or use to another; deflect; to give pleasure to especially by distracting the attention from what burdens or distresses. And finally, it defines 'distraction' as: the act of distracting or the state of being distracted, especially mental confusion; something that distracts; amusement.

So the purpose of distractions is to hinder you or keep you from reaching your destination; and to bring about mental confusion. We can clearly tell who the author of distractions is: your adversary, the devil.

7.1 Detours

However, in meditating on this subject, I noticed another word that begins with 'd' we sometimes confuse as being the enemy, when we are actually fighting with God (and divine purpose). That word is 'detour'.

Have you ever been rushing to get someplace, and to your amazement (or better yet, bewilderment) the 'normal' route of travel has a detour? This doesn't mean that you won't arrive at your destination, but that an alternate route (one that you didn't choose) has to be taken. While on the detour, be diligent to follow the road signs to bring you back on course.

Again, lets backup and define 'detour' in the American Heritage dictionary as: a deviation from a direct course or the usual procedure; especially a roundabout way temporarily replacing part of a route. The difference between distractions and detours is that a distraction is designed to keep you from your destination. Yet a detour is designed to complete your destination (in spite of obstacles or issues in your way).

A classic biblical example of a detour is the children of Israel being delivered out of Egypt (see Exodus 13:17-18 below). There was a more direct route than the one God led them on, but God knew that there was more at stake than them just arriving at a destination. There were life lessons that a foundation was being laid for – for them to trust God in spite of what they saw (or thought they knew).

> (Exodus 13:17-18) When Pharaoh let the people go, God led them not by way of the land of the Philistines, although that was nearer; for God said, Lest the people change their purpose when they see war and return to Egypt. But God led the people around by way of the wilderness toward the Red Sea. And the Israelites went up marshaled [in ranks] out of the land of Egypt.

Have you experienced some seemingly round-about wandering in your life? The way to deal with this is to stay seeking God and following after Him. He has all the plans for your life and will reveal them to you step by step; from faith to faith.

Remember we are talking about *obedience*. Now why would God reveal steps #13, 14, and 15 to you and you haven't even been *obedient* with steps #3, 4, and 5? Then we get frustrated and think God is mad with us. No, He isn't, He is just patiently waiting for you to be *obedient* in the step (phase) that you are in so that He can reveal the next step (phase) to you.

I want to look at Joseph, and his story will lead us into our next biblical illustration. Joseph had a dream, yet it took almost 22 years until he actually saw the dream in the natural. He had gone through a great "detour" in route to this dream, but in his discourse on the matter, he said:

> (Genesis 45:5) But now, do not be distressed and disheartened or vexed and angry with yourselves because you sold me here, **for God sent me ahead of you to preserve life**.

His journey to his dream was mis-understood, he was mistreated by those closest to him. Yet he did not take it personal, yet through time and his journey, he realized that God sent him, and his brothers were simply the occasion (or the thorn) that catapulted or directed (detoured if you will) him into purpose.

7.2   *Thorns*
Speaking of thorns, let us examine this next *portion* of scripture:

(1 Corinthians 12:7-10) And to keep me from being puffed up and too much elated by the exceeding greatness (preeminence) of these revelations, there was given me a thorn (a splinter) in the flesh, a messenger of Satan, to rack and buffet and harass me, to keep me from being excessively exalted. [8] Three times I called upon the Lord and besought [Him] about this and begged that it might depart from me; [9] But He said to me, My grace (My favor and loving-kindness and mercy) is enough for you [sufficient against any danger and enables you to bear the trouble manfully]; for My strength and power are made perfect (fulfilled and completed) and show themselves most effective in [your] weakness. Therefore, I will all the more gladly glory in my weaknesses and infirmities, that the strength and power of Christ (the Messiah) may rest (yes, may pitch a tent over and dwell) upon me! [10] So for the sake of Christ, I am well pleased and take pleasure in infirmities, insults, hardships, persecutions, perplexities and distresses; for when I am weak [in human strength], then am I [truly] strong (able, powerful in divine strength).

Actually, I need to share with you a foundation of how this scripture came alive to me personally. While in Tulsa Oklahoma attending school, I would go to the library and check out books weekly. I was hungry for the things of God and knew that I needed a deeper understanding. I knew that in and of myself I could not accomplish what God had in store for me, yet He had led me to this school with access to all this information of others that had walked similar walks. So I was on a serious "glean" mission. As Ruth, I was gleaning "handfuls on purpose" and storing it up for future reference.

Let me detour for a moment and drop a nugget about Ruth (see Ruth chapter 2). In studying, I found out that she gleaned enough each day for 3 days of food for her and her mother-in-law, and she gleaned for 3 harvest seasons. She was diligent to go daily and glean, and to prepare what she had received. This is what I was doing there at Rhema Bible Training College (RBTC). I had "happened" upon the field (I was exposed to the ministry from a book by Dad Hagin that I bought in a thrift store – I was hungry and God fed me) – and I was diligent to continue to glean (reap) and store up. I had fellow classmates that joked about me attending "Paulette 101" classes with the Holy Spirit as my Teacher.

Now back to the reference of the thorn, I read a book in the RBTC library by Charles Capps titled "The Messenger of Satan" based on this scripture in 1 Corinthians 12. It was after reading this book that I noticed the "thorn" was referring to people. I made a personal connection that the greatest thorns are the people who are closest to you. I heard someone say that proximity breeds contention and contempt. Yes, I can say that I have learned this personally.

One of the reasons that God showed me this was to remind me to be thankful and grateful for His selection and appointment (and anointing), yet to never forget from whence I came. I definitely felt like a weak vessel and not qualified to handle the things of God because I was not brought up in the church. But God's strength was made perfect in my weakness, because He did not have to strip so much tradition from me to get me prepared to be a vessel of worthy use:

> (2 Timothy 2:20) But in a great house there are not only vessels of gold and silver, but also [utensils] of wood and earthenware, and some for honorable and noble [use] and some for menial and ignoble [use].

Like Joseph, it wasn't all a wonderful walk. My family did not sell me into slavery, or even willfully mistreat me. But some of the situations that occurred in my life drove me to seek God even more, and kept me close to God. These events made it so that I will not rely on myself, or my family, but on God. These "thorn" roles in my spiritual development was a "detour" and not a "distraction".

Yet there are "thorns" that are of a combination "distraction and detour," based on disobedience. The children of Israel were told to drive out the inhabitants of the land and leave none living. But they were disobedient to the covenant, so the idolatrous nations would be thorns to the Israelites. Observe the recount of the instructions:

> (Joshua 23:6-11) So be very courageous and steadfast to keep and do all that is written in the Book of the Law of Moses, turning not aside from it to the right hand or the left, [7] That you may not mix with these nations that remain among you, or make mention of the

names of their gods or swear by them or serve them or bow down to them. [8] But cling to the Lord your God as you have done to this day. [9] For the Lord has driven out from before you great and strong nations; and as for you, no man has been able to withstand you to this day. [10] One man of you shall put to flight a thousand, for it is the Lord your God Who fights for you, as He promised you. [11] Be very watchful of yourselves, therefore, to love the Lord your God.

I found a footnote in the amplified bible for this section that illustrates the importance of being obedient to the instructions of the covenant:

> Everything depended on whether or not Israel would continue to be faithful to the covenant. Joshua's words do not conceal his apprehension. Seven times he refers to the idolatrous nations still left in Canaan. He knew the snare they would be to Israel, and he therefore prescribed three safeguards.
>
> - First, there must be brave adherence to God's word (Joshua 23:6).
> - Second, there must be a vigilantly continued separation from the Canaanite nations (Joshua 23:7).
> - Finally, there must be a cleaving to the Lord with real and fervent love (Joshua 23:8-11).

7.3 *Speed-bump or brick-wall?*

You probably have wondered why I titled this section "Speed-bump or Brick-wall"? Well, I have an answer for you. Distractions and detours can be handled as a speed-bump in your journey, where you slow down to go over it, but it doesn't stop you from arriving at your destination. In studying the Public Works process, speed-bumps are installed for safety reasons – for the safety of pedestrians and other users of the streets (installed mostly in residential areas and parking lots). In the spirit realm, I see speed-bumps as a way that God has us walk out the word of God in our life, yet remain attached in our environment. To allow us to be observant, as well obedient to the set laws (rules) in the natural realm as well as the spiritual.

Now the brick-walls – that is self-explanatory. If you are driving or running and you hit a brick-wall, that can be pretty painful and or destructive. The attitude of our heart that we maintain while dealing with distractions and detours is the marker for how we are handling the situation. Meaning if we look at it as a speed-bump or a brick-wall; the wrong attitude means we see it as a brick-wall. This will require the renewal of our attitude (mind) with the word of God to continue on the journey.

7.4 *Busy distractions*

For the next *portion*, I'd like to look in on two of my sisters, Mary and Martha.

> (Luke 10:38-42) Now while they were on their way, it occurred that Jesus entered a certain village, and a woman named Martha

received and welcomed Him into her house. ³⁹ And she had a sister named Mary, who seated herself at the Lord's feet and was listening to His teaching. ⁴⁰ But Martha [overly occupied and too busy] was distracted with much serving; and she came up to Him and said, Lord, is it nothing to You that my sister has left me to serve alone? Tell her then to help me [to lend a hand and do her part along with me]! ⁴¹ But the Lord replied to her by saying, Martha, Martha, you are anxious and troubled about many things; ⁴² There is need of only one or but a few things. Mary has chosen the good *portion* [that which is to her advantage], which shall not be taken away from her.

How many of us are 'troubled about many things', yet missing the opportunity of a lifetime to receive from Jesus? Yes, there is work to be done in the house (church), but here was the manifested presence of God in the house, yet Martha allowed her serving work to be a brick-wall instead of a bridge.

I am speaking to the hearts of those serving in ministry in any form or fashion. Please, please, please stay sensitive to the Spirit of God, not the program, and be a faithful servant. It is good and appropriate to have a plan (a program), but when Jesus shows up on the scene, HE IS THE PROGRAM!!! So take your place at His feet in His presence.

As I am writing this and thinking of my own Martha-type service, as well others, I can see how we get caught up in 'is it nothing…I'm left to serve alone'. Martha, being the great hostess that she was, detail oriented, and a woman of excellence, she may not have been adhering to her daily devotionals. Yet Mary was. So when the very presence of God came in the room with answers and clarity to Mary's devotions and study time, she stopped everything to receive. But to Martha, Mary was being lazy and non-helpful. We must be careful not to judge other's service to God. You may not understand why Sister Whatchaname loses it every time the service gets to a certain spot, but Jesus sees and knows; and will reward accordingly. Know this, He will not accept anything of the flesh. So Mary make sure you are worshipping in spirit and in truth, not just in a feeling. Because the truth of the matter is there is work to be done, so don't waste precious time in the flesh.

I would just like to lay out some biblical examples of the types of distractions we will face while on assignment:

Example One – Everyday stuff:

> (Mark 4:19-20) Then the cares and anxieties of the world and <u>distractions</u> of the age, and the pleasure and delight and false glamour and deceitfulness of riches, and the craving and passionate desire for other things creep in and choke and suffocate the Word, and it becomes fruitless. [20] And those sown on the good (well-adapted) soil are the ones who hear the Word and receive and accept and welcome it and bear fruit—some thirty times as much as was sown, some sixty times as

much, and some [even] a hundred times as much.

Example Two – Marital status:

> (1 Corinthians 7:32-35) My desire is to have you <u>free from all anxiety and distressing care</u>. The unmarried man is anxious about the things of the Lord—how he may please the Lord; ^{33} But the married man is anxious about worldly matters—how he may please his wife—^{34} And he is drawn in diverging directions [his interests are divided and he is distracted from his devotion to God]. And the unmarried woman or girl is concerned and anxious about the matters of the Lord, how to be wholly separated and set apart in body and spirit; but the married woman has her cares [centered] in earthly affairs—how she may please her husband. ^{35} Now I say this for your own welfare and profit, not to put [a halter of] restraint upon you, but to promote what is seemly and in good order and to secure your undistracted and undivided devotion to the Lord.

This is why marriage must be centered in Christ because a 3-fold cord is not easily broken and with Him as the center the devotions are not divided between the things of God and this world. This is how we avoid this distraction and keep it from being a brick wall, only a speed bump that we slow down to go over.

Example Three – God disciplines His sons:

> (Hebrews 12:6-7) For the Lord corrects and disciplines everyone whom He loves, and He punishes, even scourges, every son whom He accepts and welcomes to His heart and cherishes. ⁷ You must submit to and endure [correction] for discipline; God is dealing with you as with sons. For what son is there whom his father does not [thus] train and correct and discipline?

The distraction is when we murmur and complain in the process and prolong the lesson – or never learn it. God's disciplines are not distractions, but detours because He knows what we need and when we need it, as well as things we do not need. We make this a brick wall when we do not accept or welcome his chastening or discipline.

CHAPTER 8 – PRAYER & FASTING

8.1   Warrior

> (Psalm 144:1-2, 15) BLESSED BE the Lord, my Rock and my keen and firm Strength, Who **teaches my hands to war and my fingers to fight**—² My Steadfast Love and my Fortress, my High Tower and my Deliverer, my Shield and He in Whom I trust and take refuge, Who subdues my people under me…¹⁵ Happy and blessed are the people who are in such a case; yes, happy (blessed, fortunate, prosperous, to be envied) are the people whose God is the Lord!

Psalm 144 is titled 'the warrior's psalm' and it is an appropriate beginning point for this chapter. But let me define warrior just in case people are wondering if I am talking to them or not. The first definition is a man engaged or experienced in warfare; and the second definition is a person engaged in some struggle or conflict. The day you accepted Christ you became a warrior of the Faith and a soldier in God's army. Notice I said "the Faith," the Faith is as the amplified bible puts it "the leaning of your whole personality on God in complete trust and *obedience*" (see 1 Thessalonians 3:7 AMP); and as "your conviction respecting man's relationship to God and divine things, keeping the trust and holy fervor born of faith and a part of it" (see 1 Corinthians 16:13). Also, re-read chapter one on Jesus Faith to understand the warfare that may manifest.

(2 Timothy 2:3-4) Take [with me] your share of the hardships and suffering [which you are called to endure] as a good (first-class) soldier of Christ Jesus. [4] No soldier when in service gets entangled in the enterprises of [civilian] life; his aim is to satisfy and please the one who enlisted him.

We are promised tribulation and hardships by the Lord Jesus Christ Himself, so we would benefit from learning how to share and endure them with fellow soldiers. Avoiding the entanglements of this world, those that we just discussed in the previous chapter, that can distract us from the spiritual battle that we are engaged in. Why would we willingly choose to go AWOL (absent without leave) from God who has enlisted us in this battle? We didn't choose Him, He chose us, and equips us for the battle (John 15:16).

A few suggested authors on prayer and warfare are: Dr. Myles Munroe, Dutch Sheets, Judy Jacobs, Arthur Murray, Cindy Trimm, Kimberley Daniels, Ida Ullrich, C. Peter Wagner, Larry Lee, Cindy Jacobs, Cherri Fuller, Fuschia Pinkett, Kenneth Hagin (Jr & Sr) just to name a few – but there is good material out there to help us know how to pray effectively and fervently. Since we do not wrestle with flesh and blood (see Ephesians 6 and 2 Corinthians 10), this battle takes place with pulling down imaginations (thoughts – strongholds) and standing on the word of God in our thoughts. We will talk more about this in the fasting section of this chapter.

8.2   *Dressed For Battle*
I want to begin this section with a rather large section of scripture. I have added emphasis to the text with bold and

underlining and will go into further detail of what is meant by this. Ephesians 6:10-18

> ^{10} In conclusion, be strong in the Lord [be empowered through your union with Him]; draw your strength from Him [that strength which His boundless might provides]. ^{11} Put on God's whole armor [**the armor of a heavy-armed soldier which God supplies**], that you may be able successfully to stand up against [all] the strategies and the deceits of the de'Il. ^{12} For we are **not wrestling with flesh and blood** [contending only with physical opponents], but against the despotisms, against the powers, against [the master spirits who are] the world rulers of this present darkness, against the spirit forces of wickedness in the heavenly (supernatural) sphere. ^{13} **Therefore put on God's complete armor**, that you may be able to resist and stand your ground on the evil day [of danger], and, having done all [the crisis demands], to stand [firmly in your place]. ^{14} Stand therefore [hold your ground], having tightened the belt of truth around your loins and having put on the breastplate of integrity and of moral rectitude and right standing with God, ^{15} And having shod your feet in preparation [to face the enemy with the firm-footed stability, the promptness, and the readiness produced by the good news] of the Gospel of peace. ^{16} Lift up over all the [covering] shield of saving faith, upon which you can quench all the flaming missiles of the wicked [one]. ^{17} And take the helmet of salvation and the sword that the Spirit wields, which is the Word of God. ^{18} **Pray at all**

times (on every occasion, in every season) **in the Spirit**, with all [manner of] prayer and entreaty. To that end keep alert and watch with strong purpose and perseverance, interceding in behalf of all the saints (God's consecrated people).

The few points that I want to draw out here are found first in verse 11 – the armor of a heavy armed soldier which God supplies –we see that He equips us for the battle. This equipping is in our thinking, our soulish realm, the area that houses our mind/ will/ emotions/ intellect/ thoughts/ reasoning/ imaginations/ personality/ memories/ conscious – this is the battleground, and we have been given all that is needed to successfully engage in this battle. We have the mind of Christ (1 Corinthians 2:16) and must grow in understanding His mind through spending time in the word of God and in prayer. Verse 12 lets us see that we are not wrestling with flesh and blood, but it is a spiritual battle. The enemy loves to attack the battlefield of the mind, especially with believers who talk the talk, but don't walk the walk. We must get a better understanding of how to effectively put on this armor and do battle. Verse 13 says that we must put on God's complete armor and verse 18 says to pray at all times. AT ALL TIMES, not sometimes, not just when things are going good, or when things are going bad – but at all times. This does not mean that we go around being spooky with prayer all day long, it just means that we constantly keep in mind that we are in a spiritual battle that never retreats.

We are to put on the WHOLE armor, not just bits and pieces. One piece without the other will not work in this spiritual battle that we are in. We can get seriously hurt or injure numerous people if we are not properly adorned in prayer and in life. The armor is important, but we must prioritize how we obtain the understanding of this armor.

Matthew 6:33 can help us put on this armor. *"But seek first his kingdom and his righteousness, and all these things will be given to you as well."* These things added was talking about clothes and eating; doesn't that sound a little like armor and feeding your spirit man the proper diet? To those who are concerned that they just don't know how to put on the armor of God: just seek the kingdom (God's way of doing things) and the armor will be given to you. Seek a better understanding of truth and righteousness, so the belt and breastplate will remain on you. Do it daily. Seek a more intimate understanding of the peace of God – keep your mind stayed on Him. Continue to lean your whole personality on God in complete trust and confidence which is true faith; that will empower your shield of faith to quench the darts of the enemy. Anoint your shield of faith with the oil of the Holy Spirit. A verse from a song that helped me understand this principle said: "nobody ever told me there wouldn't be dents in my armor, but He promised me my armor would always work."

Continue in the joy of the Lord which is your strength because God (and His kingdom) are able to restore the joy of your salvation. It is called the 'helmet' of salvation – it covers your natural ability to think. At salvation you received the mind of Christ – now think on these things. As you seek the kingdom you will better learn how to use your sword of the spirit which is the word of God. Keep in mind we are talking about prayer.

Don't get me wrong, as a baby saint (an immature saint, newly saved, etc.) you do have this armor – but you must seek the Lord for how to properly function with these pieces. Your armor may not look like everybody else's armor – at least not at first. Look at David in his first public battle. He didn't rely on looking the part, but on the God of Israel's power and the tools he had practiced with during his daily seeking. But there was an elevation of armor because we never hear of David going back to the sling shot; he took Goliath's sword and began learning to use armor. The point is he began where he was, then grew because of his intimate understanding of God, being a man after God's heart.

Notice He gave nothing for the back part of the armor here in Ephesians 6? It is because God is our rear guard (as in Isaiah 58:8 which we will discuss in a moment), He covers you supernaturally as well as through others in battle with you.

We must be clothed in righteousness first – put on the robe of righteousness before any of this armor can be effective because according to Isaiah 64 in the amplified: *our best attempt at righteousness is as filthy rags.* Soldiers would have on clothing beneath the armor, it was a robe like thing that was between them and the armor – this is the robe of righteousness. Righteousness has benefits, look at Proverbs chapters 10 and 11, both chapters are packed full of the benefits of righteousness, and the opposite as well.

As warriors dressed for battle, we then engage in the matter of addressing strongholds. Strongholds can be godly or evil; we must erect godly strongholds and tear down ungodly and evil strongholds. The first definition of what we are pulling down, according to Edgardo Silvoso, is "a mindset impregnated with hopelessness that causes the believer to accept as unchangeable something that he/she knows is contrary to the will of God." We have to tear down these bad thoughts and wrong thinking in prayer. The second definition of what we are pulling down, from Joyce Meyer, is "a house of mental thoughts built at an early age, for future occupation by demonic forces." We see we are going in the spirit realm in prayer and bull dozing some bad thinking that was set up long ago. We pull them down, according to 2 Corinthians 10:4-5, and we erect the strongholds of the Lord such as: the Lord is my refuge, my strong tower, my shield and buckler, He is for me, who can be against me. Here are a few reference scriptures for you to see this on your own in the word: Psalm 27:1, 37:39; Isaiah 25:4; Jeremiah 16:19; and Nahum 1:7.

8.3   Fasting

Isaiah 58 is a good place to begin when talking about fasting. The chapter is titled well in several versions of the bible: God's kind of fast; true fasting; right and wrong fasting. But when I read it for the first time, I never saw the mention of not eating? Or even the "how to" of fasting food? I surmised that it must be the principles that God wants us to get first, and He will empower us on the techniques as we go forward.

> (Isaiah 58:4-5) [The facts are that] you fast only for strife and debate and to smite with the fist of wickedness. Fasting as you do today will not cause your voice to be heard on high. ⁵ Is such a fast as yours what I have chosen, a day for a man to humble himself with sorrow in his soul? [Is true fasting merely mechanical?] Is it only to bow down his head like a bulrush and to spread sackcloth and ashes under him [to indicate a condition of heart that he does not have]? Will you call this a fast and an acceptable day to the Lord?

We see here that God is not after the mechanics of fasting, but that He is looking at what is going on in our heart. Verse 6 and 7 go on to talk about the fast that God is seeking or has chosen:

(Isaiah 58:6-7) [Rather] is not this the fast that I have chosen: to loose the bonds of wickedness, to undo the bands of the yoke, to let the oppressed go free, and that you break every [enslaving] yoke? ⁷ Is it not to divide your bread with the hungry and bring the homeless poor into your house—when you see the naked, that you cover him, and that you hide not yourself from [the needs of] your own flesh and blood?

Do we see food mentioned here? I don't. He is looking at our hearts, we should be crying out for this to take place, in ourselves, and in the people whom we are praying and fasting for. And here are some benefits of fasting:

(Isaiah 58:8, 11) Then shall your light break forth like the morning, and **your healing (your restoration and the power of a new life)** shall spring forth speedily; your righteousness (your rightness, your justice, and your right relationship with God) shall go before you [conducting you to peace and prosperity], and **the glory of the Lord shall be your rear guard.**

¹¹ And **the Lord shall guide you continually and satisfy you** in drought and in dry places and make strong your bones. And **you shall be like a watered garden** and like a spring of water whose waters fail not.

Those are some exciting benefits! And good reasons to fast and seek God! Look at that in verse 8, His glory will be our rear guard! That is why there is no part of the armor for our back in Ephesians 6 that we looked at above, because He has our back! And we solidify this by fasting and praying. One last point I would like to pull out here is:

> (Isaiah 58:9-10) Then you shall call, and the Lord will answer; you shall cry, and He will say, Here I am. If you take away from your midst yokes of oppression [wherever you find them], the finger pointed in scorn [toward the oppressed or the godly], and every form of false, harsh, unjust, and wicked speaking, [10] And if you pour out that with which you sustain your own life for the hungry and satisfy the need of the afflicted, then shall your light rise in darkness, and your obscurity and gloom become like the noonday.

Verse 9 shows the relationship between true fasting and answered prayer. Verse 10 says why we should be giving up food, it can be looked at like intercession or standing in the gap, whether for ourselves, or for others.

Fasting does not move God, but denies the flesh, and if done properly, strengthens the spirit man. We need to be sure that we fast with purpose – not just being hungry or on a diet, but have a desired outcome; have text to meditate on. Allow the natural hunger pains to be reminders to pray, to stir up the spirit, to meditate on the chosen text and the purpose of the fast. We can also incorporate fasting from wrong thoughts, this is why it is important to know the word, to study it and get it in your heart so that when wrong thoughts enter your head, you can let those wrong thoughts be a reminder of your purpose in life – which is to glorify God, and fulfill every *assignment* He has given you.

A few years ago, Pastor Gregory Dickow had a season of fasting wrong thoughts daily. He said we have no use for wrong thoughts. Our physical, emotional, spiritual body does not need them, but our natural body does need natural food – so choosing to fast unhealthy thoughts can be more beneficial than a food fast. Replace the wrong (unscriptural) thoughts with the truths and promises of the word. This will increase and develop your faith in the process. The program he did was for the 40-day Lent season, but the response was so great that he continued it again; and eventually turned this "idea" into a devotional book. I participated and it changed my life because it changed my thinking and boosted my prayer life. I am not promoting a person, but a principle on fasting. Yes, a food fast is still needed and has a place, but those wrong thoughts have no place and we can do this throughout our lives. Try it.

> (Luke 5:33-35) Then they said to Him, The disciples of John practice fasting often and offer up prayers of [special] petition, and so do [the disciples] of the Pharisees also, but Yours eat and drink. [34] And Jesus said to them, Can you make the wedding guests fast as long as the bridegroom is with them? [35] But the days will come when the bridegroom will be taken from them; and then they will fast in those days.

When you spend time in His presence, He will empower you, which is far better than a food fast. But when He is gone, as Jesus said here in Luke 5, then you will fast to get back into His presence per say. Also, because Jesus promised to never leave nor forsake us, constant fasting may not be needed. But if you sense that He is not as near as He once was, maybe fasting would be a good idea to clear your spiritual eyes and ears to see and hear from Him clearly?

Individual fasting is important, and then there are times that the Lord will call for a corporate fast; where all the people are working on their hearts and their relationship with God to bring about the desired purpose of the fast. Some examples of corporate fasting are those of Esther, Ezra, and Nehemiah. Here is a good example of what individual as well as corporate fasting can do:

> (Joel 2:12-15) Therefore also now, says the Lord, turn and keep on coming to Me with all your heart, with fasting, with weeping, and with mourning [until every hindrance is removed and the broken fellowship is restored]. [13] Rend your hearts and not your garments and return to the Lord, your God, for He is gracious and merciful, slow to anger, and abounding in loving-kindness; and He revokes His sentence of evil [when His conditions are met]. [14] Who knows but what He will turn, revoke your sentence [of evil], and leave a blessing behind Him [giving you the means with which to serve Him], even a cereal or meal offering and a drink offering for the Lord, your God? [15] Blow the trumpet in Zion; set apart a fast [a day of restraint and humility]; call a solemn assembly.

8.4   A Consecrated Life

I have heard of the Daniel fast, yet I was corrected recently that this was not a fast, but a lifestyle. I began to refer to it as a consecration to the Lord using the principles which Daniel lived by for eating, and time with God. Personally, I do this more than fasting because as the head of my household it is difficult to do a complete fast and still function in our culture today. But there are times that I will fast for a day or three days, taking only water (and juice if needed). I prefer to just live a fasted lifestyle – meaning I don't overindulge or fully satisfy my flesh with its appetite desires. You know how you will have a taste for something? I will acknowledge the craving, and then deny my flesh the satisfaction of fulfilling it – just to remind the flesh who is in control. This is all part of living a life consecrated unto the Lord and not giving in to the dictates of the flesh and the worldly system.

> (Daniel 1:8, 17, 20) [8] But Daniel determined in his heart that he would not defile himself by [eating his portion of] the king's rich and dainty food or by [drinking] the wine which he drank; therefore he requested of the chief of the eunuchs that he might [be allowed] not to defile himself...
>
> [17] As for these four youths, God gave them knowledge and skill in all learning and wisdom, and Daniel had understanding in all [kinds of] visions and dreams...[20] And in all matters of wisdom and understanding concerning which the king asked them, he found them ten times better than all the [learned] magicians and enchanters who were in his whole realm...

These are good principles to live by, to set our hearts after God to not defile ourselves. Not denying food but denying the principles of the world (the king's dainty food) and walking in covenant with God. It is not about fasting, but about lifestyle. So doing a 10 or 21 day "Daniel Consecration" can assist us to make sure that we keep our hearts determined to please God – which is eating only fruits and vegetables, juice and water, and some type of protein – just denying myself meat, carbohydrates, sweets and soda. Another benefit of this consecration is that it is training us to be mindful of the things of the world. Whenever I would crave or want meat or pastries and stuff, it would just remind me to make sure my heart is set on God. It brings flesh denial and spiritual reminders of why we are here in the first place.

8.5   Pray, pray, PRAY...

I titled this section 'Pray, pray, PRAY' simply to mean pray without ceasing. Pray out of habit, pray out of relationship building, pray supplications and intercessions for others and yourself. Just pray, because we know that *the earnest effectual fervent prayer of the righteous makes tremendous power available, dynamic in its working, is powerful and effective and is something to be reckoned with, and produces wonderful results* (James 5:16 AMP. KJV, NIV, MSG, NLT).

The topic of prayer and lifestyle unto God was so important that Paul addressed it in his pastoral epistle to Timothy, a young pastor of a growing church:

> (1 Timothy 2:8) I desire therefore that in every place men should pray, without anger or quarreling or resentment or doubt [in their minds], lifting up holy hands.

Male and female, God created mankind (Genesis 1:26), and we are to all be praying without ceasing. The consecrated lifestyle will help us to rid ourselves of anger, quarreling, and resentment in our minds. As we spend time in God's presence, He will show us how to properly deal with those things in our mind and thinking. He will do as the psalmist said *create in me a new heart and a right spirit* (Psalm

51:10). And it is as we pray in every season and on every occasion (as discussed earlier in Ephesians 6:18), that we grow in our understanding of who God is and who we are in Him and our ability to pray and access heaven on earth. As in the model prayer in Matthew 6:10, we are to be daily praying and accessing heaven to have it manifest here on earth. We should be walking in forgiveness daily and asking for help with temptation daily because this is as the text says *the kingdom and the power and the glory forever. Amen.* (Matthew 6:12-18). So Pray, pray, PRAY always.

CHAPTER 9 – RECONCILING THE HEARTS

To reconcile is to restore to friendship or harmony; to change from enmity (or strife) to friendship; to settle; to resolve. God's desire is to bring forth this type of reconciliation.

I must give a disclaimer at the beginning of this chapter, there will be a heavy amount of scriptures quoted but this is necessary to establish the bottom line principle that God desires to reconcile the hearts and bring a flock of men to the body of Christ and the overall kingdom of God.

9.1   Malachi 4

> (Malachi 4:4-6) [Earnestly] remember the law of Moses, My servant, the statutes and the ordinances which I commanded him on [Mount] Horeb [to give] to all Israel. [5] Behold, I will send you Elijah the prophet before the great and terrible day of the Lord comes. [6] And he shall turn and reconcile the hearts of the [estranged] fathers to the [ungodly] children, and the hearts of the [rebellious] children to [the piety of] their fathers **[a reconciliation produced by repentance of the ungodly]**, lest I come and smite the land with a curse and a ban of utter destruction.

So much is contained in these last 3 verses of Malachi and of the Old Testament. I will just jump in and begin with verse 6, reconcile the hearts – in the soulish realm, to be renewed to the word in our thinking, and as mentioned in the end of chapter 8, to receive that new heart and begin to walk through life declaring what thus says the Lord about His people. Also notice that the amplified refers to the children and the fathers and says that repentance must take place. The text says "I shall turn" – God is orchestrating and turning the hearts of His people to bring about this reconciliation, but *obedience* is needed. *Obedience* to the nudging at the heart. Notice the last *portion* of verse 6 says "lest I come and smite…" – this is almost like a promise if reconciliation does not take place. Some, both men and children, feel like there is a curse following them –another area to examine for the cause is rebelliousness and ungodliness (as mentioned here in verse 6). We are all called the sons (or children) of God, we must be reconciled unto God so we must be doing our part in evangelism. Evangelism is sowing seed and watering seed so that God can provide the increase. He said that "I shall turn and reconcile the hearts," so He is doing His part, we must do our part.

9.2 Our part
Our part is described well in the following text:

> (Deuteronomy 4:9-10) Only take heed, and guard your life diligently, lest you forget the things which your eyes have seen and lest they depart from your [mind and] heart all the days of your life. Teach them to your children and your children's children—[10] Especially how on the day that you stood before the Lord your God in Horeb, the Lord said to me, Gather the people together to Me and I will make them hear My words, that they may learn [reverently] to fear Me all the days they

live upon the earth and that they may teach their children.

We are to pass down the word of God and right living to our children and our children's children. The enemy is attacking the men to cause major breeches in this process. It is not that the devil does not like you, he does not like God and will do whatever he can in an attempt to defeat Him.

We will teach the children, the next generation – it is a basic thing, but we must tell our children that God loves them; instill the love of God in them. God is our heavenly Father, our teacher, our guardian and He is the best example of how we are to be guides and guardians to the next generation.

> (Psalm 103:17) But the mercy and lovingkindness of the Lord are from everlasting to everlasting upon those who reverently and worshipfully fear Him, and His righteousness is to children's children—

We will reverence, honor and fear the Lord our God. In so doing, we leave an inheritance for our children and our children's children.

> (Psalm 128:4-6) Behold, thus shall the man be blessed who reverently and worshipfully fears the Lord. [5] May the Lord bless you out of Zion [His sanctuary], and may you see the

> prosperity of Jerusalem all the days of your life; ⁶ Yes, may you see your children's children. Peace be upon Israel!

We will have the peace resting upon our children. We will leave an inheritance for the next generation; an inheritance of godliness and so much more.

> (Proverbs 13:22) A good man leaves an inheritance [of moral stability and goodness] to his children's children, and the wealth of the sinner [finds its way eventually] into the hands of the righteous, for whom it was laid up.

We must teach our children, and do what is pleasing to God, because this text shows that the wealth we need to advance the kingdom is just waiting on us to do the first *portion* of this text, to teach our children, that the wealth be transferred to the righteous that it was prepared for all along. Tying this all into the chapter topic, the enemy has launched a relentless assault on the men (the fathers) to live outside of the will of God, leaving the women (the mothers) to stand in the gap of something we were not designed to do. The man is designed to be the head of the family, and the woman is designed help him meet the purposes of God. The woman has purposes as well, but do you see the strategy of the enemy to remove the man, which hinders the purpose of woman.

Notice that the reconciliation according to this text is in the fathers and the children with no mention of the mothers –

this was probably a forward look of so many mothers standing in the gap raising the children. ALL must walk in and ask forgiveness which brings reconciliation. But then we all have the ministry of reconciliation as Paul describes in 2 Corinthians 5:18, and the amplified bible adds *"that by word and deed we might aim to bring others into harmony with Him."* So we must be mindful to not only say, but do and be who God has called us to be in this season – it is part of the ministry of reconciliation.

I need the readers to know that my heart is heavy as I write this because society has made it acceptable for men to produce children and leave the mother the full responsibility of raising that child. God never designed it to be this way, yet He has given grace unto mothers and children all across the land to show that His strength is made perfect in our weakness as we are called to do something we were not designed to do.

The enemy thinks he is succeeding at ravaging the next generation, but God has people that will stand on His word, that will speak it, and live it, and it will come to past. There is a reconciliation coming that only God can bring about, yet we must be diligent in doing our part. Another society issue that adds onto this blight in our spiritual inheritance is that our young women are being taught (if not directly, by the lack thereof) that they do not need a man to be successful. This is a terrible mindset (stronghold) that must be torn down because it can cause women to enable men to not rise up and take their rightful places. I ask the Lord to remove the blinders from the eyes of His people that we see this as bad thinking and get in line with the word of God – because this warped mindset hinders the purposes of God. To add to those warped mindsets is the fact that we are teaching a double standard to the young boys and girls – that it is okay for a boy to have loose standards, but not for a girl? Does that make any sense? It is a set up for failure, a disguise of the enemy to keep families from coming together.

Another point to draw from the above text (Malachi 4:5) is that of the day of the Lord. I researched several different sources in an attempt to better understand what this meant. Varying explanations are out there, but for the purpose of this chapter and the principle being established I will only share the following excerpt from the Holman Illustrated Bible Dictionary:

> ...the day of the Lord is thus aimed at warning sinners among God's people of the danger of trusting in traditional religion without commitment to God and His way of life...and is thus a point in time in which God displays His sovereign initiative to reveal His control of history, of time, of His people, and of all people.

So we can see that the day of the Lord is not really for the people who truly believe in God and have received the Lord Jesus Christ as savior; but for those around who put on a show like as if they really have accepted this redemption, yet are not truly committed to God and His way of life. Honestly, with society the way that it is now, I truly feel like the day of the Lord is around the corner, but people have been saying this for hundreds of years. The bottom line is our goal is to assist the Lord, as co-laborers with Christ, in reconciling the hearts of the fathers and the children. Notice it refers to "fathers" not just "men," because many men are in denial and are not fully accepting the responsibility of father, provider, disciplinarian, lover (of the child), guardian, or caregiver. Look around in most churches, the women out number the men – and many people wonder why? As a woman and mother myself this can be very frustrating, but I know that the Lord is up to something and this text shows me that He will get the glory out of this.

Let's go to our next text, we will tie them all together by the end of this chapter:

> (Matthew 1:18-25 NIV emphasis added) This is how the birth of Jesus Christ came about: His mother Mary was pledged to be married to **Joseph**, but before they came together, she was found to be with child through the Holy Spirit. [19] Because **Joseph her husband was a righteous man** and did not want to expose her to public disgrace, he had in mind to divorce her quietly. [20] But after he had considered this, an angel of the Lord appeared to him in a dream and said, "Joseph son of David, do not be afraid to take Mary home as your wife, because what is conceived in her is from the Holy Spirit. [21] She will give birth to a son, and you are to give him the name Jesus, because he will save his people from their sins." [22] All this took place to fulfill what the Lord had said through the prophet: [22] "The virgin will be with child and will give birth to a son, and they will call him Immanuel"—which means, "God with us." [24] When Joseph woke up, he did what

the angel of the Lord had commanded him and took Mary home as his wife. [25] But he had no union with her until she gave birth to a son. And he gave him the name Jesus.

Everyone wants the "blessed and highly favored" status of Mary, but are there people willing to step up and truly be the "Joseph" of the story? Someone has to accept the *assignment* to "marry" the carrier of the "holy thing." The importance of people's *assignment* being recognized and accepted not only assists in the purpose for the individual's life, but an innumerable amount of people. Imagine if Joseph saw the responsibility and said that he did not want to assume that responsibility? No, he initially heard of the *assignment* that the person whom was espoused to him was "with child" and had decided to "put her away silently" because he did respect her, but did not fully understand the details of the *assignment*. Yet after his meeting with the angel of the Lord, he accepted the *assignment* not just in word or saying he would, but he actually united himself with Mary and began to provide for her during the "nurturing" stages of the incubation of the "holy thing." This text is a classic example of how the Lord Himself reconciled the heart of the father in Joseph to protect His plan in the earth. God is seeking men who will say yes to Him; and then not only say it (not just talk), but with corresponding actions (walk the walk).

9.3 Male Man Needed

Another Joseph in the bible is Joseph of Arimathea. There are times that we are called upon to be like the example we see in Joseph of Arimathea – he was a man of God and knew that the Lord's body needed to be taken care of. Let's look at the text and tie in this concept to the principle we have been building on in this chapter of reconciliation.

> (Mark 15:42-47 NKJV) Now when evening had come, because it was the Preparation Day, that is, the day before the Sabbath, [43] Joseph of Arimathea, a prominent council member, who was himself waiting for the kingdom of God, coming and taking courage, went in to Pilate and asked for the body of Jesus. [44] Pilate marveled that He was already dead; and summoning the centurion, he asked him if He had been dead for some time. [45] So when he found out from the centurion, he granted the body to Joseph. [46] Then he bought fine linen, took Him down, and wrapped Him in the linen. And he laid Him in a tomb which had been hewn out of the rock, and rolled a stone against the door of the tomb. [47] And Mary Magdalene and Mary the mother of Jesus observed where He was laid.)

The Lord used a man named Joseph to preserve the unborn Messiah in Matthew 1 above, and then He used another man named Joseph to watch over the body of the Messiah here in Mark 15. Both of these men were devout men, even religious men, even traditional men, but when the Lord spoke, they listened with actions following that could have endangered their lives, but they listened, took courage and had corresponding actions. These men were reconciled in their heart in their belief in the Almighty God and His leading – they are good examples for the body of Christ today.

9.4 Flock of Men

To bring a better understanding of what I am talking about, read this next *portion* of scripture and stay with me for a moment, I promise I will tie it all together and am not just rambling in circles:

> (Ezekiel 36:22-23, 31-38) Therefore say to the house of Israel, Thus says the Lord God: I do not do this for your sakes, O house of Israel, but **for My holy name's sake**, which you have profaned among the nations to which you went. [23] **And I will vindicate the holiness of My great name** and separate it for its holy purpose from all that defiles it— My name, which has been profaned among the nations, which you have profaned among them—and the nations will know, understand, and realize that I am the Lord [the Sovereign Ruler, Who calls forth loyalty and obedient service], when I shall be set apart by you and My holiness vindicated in you before their eyes and yours.
>
> ... [31] Then you shall [earnestly] remember your own evil ways and your doings that were not good, and shall loathe yourselves in your own sight for your iniquities and for your abominable deeds. [32] Not for your sake do I do this, says the Lord God; let that be known to you. Be ashamed and confounded for your [own] wicked ways, O house of Israel! [33] Thus says the Lord God: In the day that I cleanse you from all your iniquities I will [also] cause [Israel's] cities to be inhabited, and the waste places shall be rebuilt. [34] And

the desolate land shall be tilled, that which had lain desolate in the sight of all who passed by. [35] And they shall say, This land that was desolate has become like the garden of Eden, and the waste and desolate and ruined cities are fortified and inhabited. [36] Then the nations that are left round about you shall know that I the Lord have rebuilt the ruined places and replanted that which was desolate. I the Lord have spoken it, and I will do it. [37] Thus says the Lord God: For this also I will let the house of Israel inquire of Me to do it for them; **I will increase their men like a flock**. [38] Like the flock of holy things for sacrifice, like the flock of Jerusalem in her [solemn] appointed feasts, **so shall the waste cities be filled with flocks of men**; and they shall know, understand, and realize that I am the Lord [the Sovereign Ruler, Who calls forth loyalty and obedient service].

We must recognize that these cities were laid waste due to idolatry of the people and God sent word that He would do this thing. Here at the end of Ezekiel 36 we see the restoration **for God's name sake**. I am believing God for this reconciling of the hearts of men and the promised flock of men, who as the amplified bible says "realize that I am the Lord the Sovereign Ruler, Who calls forth loyalty and obedient service."

The flock of men referred to in Ezekiel is not speaking of only the male men, but the female men as well. In the opening text of this chapter both a male and a female man (Joseph and Mary) are present and had *assignments* to fulfill. Both the male and female had questions initially, but because their hearts remained hot toward the Lord, pliable and teachable, further instructions were given on how to fully walk in the *assignment* – but the ultimate choice of *obedience* is up to each individual male and female man; male and female He created man in His image. Adam and woman are a prime example in Genesis chapter 3. The woman was deceived by the conversation with the serpent (satan in disguise); it was her own choice to walk in disobedience because of the deceit sown by the enemy – giving up on her initial *assignment*. She then proceeded to share this disobedient thinking/ lifestyle with Adam; it was Adam's individual choice to disobey the law and take a shortcut to his *assignment* – which is a perfect example of why we need reconciliation.

9.5 Following God

As men of promise, we have to be mindful to not try and "help" God be God. In Genesis 16 Sarai came up with a plan to "help" God by having Abram father the promised child with Hagar her maid, and Abram listened to her plan without consulting God. This is an example of the male and female man trying to assist God, they tried to do His part and picked up an additional *assignment* in Ishmael and Hagar. I guess Abraham learned his lesson, because when the *assignments* began to clash in Genesis 21, he went to the Lord for consultation of the plan Sarah suggested to deal with the problem and God agreed with the solution – but at least Abraham consulted God first. Although the instructions were difficult and uncomfortable, Abraham had confidence to carry them out because he heard from the Lord and knew the Lord would take care of them. Both the male and female man can learn a lesson here: keep the third cord of the covenant in all major decisions. Therefore, it is on both partners to make sure they are seeking the Lord, for direction and confirmation; then following ALL of the instructions.

9.6 Fatherless

One day I was reading about the children of Israel and had an "aha" moment, if they wondered in the wilderness until everyone from that generation died (except Joshua and Caleb), that means that they all experienced grief and the loss of their parents. Yet they had to continue and go on. They had first hand experience of the scripture that says He is a father to the fatherless and a mother to the motherless.

These parentless people were given instructions as in Joshua 5 to circumcise the next generation. Circumcision of our time is no longer a physical cutting of the flesh, but a literal cutting of the heart, where we cut back the fleshly thinking in our hearts and receive the healing that God has for us (see Joshua 5). They not only received the instructions from God, but they followed them, and were empowered to live on. God took it a step further a few chapters over and renewed the covenant with His people, see Joshua 8:30-35, but we will just look at 34-35 here:

> (Joshua 8:34-35) Afterward, Joshua read all the words of the law, the blessings and cursings, all that is written in the Book of the Law. [35] There was not a word of all that Moses commanded which Joshua did not read before all the assembly of Israel, and the women, and little ones, and the foreigners who were living among them.

This chapter has discussed what it means for God to bring about reconciliation, not just in the men, but in families as a whole, which is what He began doing with creation. Our part in the matter is to continue to pass on the teaching to the next generation, whether our children or not, just to all proclaimed children of God. He equips us for our part by fulfilling His part of the matter, His word never changes, so we can stand on it. We are also preparing people for the coming day of the Lord, that the children of God not be caught off guard and un-prepared, or loose living. God is seeking a few male men that will step up to the plate as the two Joseph's discussed earlier and cover/ nourish/ nurture the *assignments* during all stages. This is not just about marriage, both Joseph preserved and protected the body of Christ – we are called to do this today. The Lord promises to bring in a flock of men for this task, not because we deserve it, but for His name's sake, and not just a rebellious group of people, but loyal people who will be obedient in service – God followers that are not trying to do it themselves, but that acknowledge Him every step of the way and be obedient to the instructions received.

CHAPTER 10 — FOR SUCH A TIME AS THIS

> (Esther 4:14-17) For if you keep silent at this time, relief and deliverance shall arise for the Jews from elsewhere, but you and your father's house will perish. And who knows but that you have come to the kingdom for such a time as this and for this very occasion? ¹⁵ Then Esther told them to give this answer to Mordecai, ¹⁶ Go, gather together all the Jews that are present in Shushan, and fast for me; and neither eat nor drink for three days, night or day. I also and my maids will fast as you do. Then I will go to the king, though it is against the law; and if I perish, I perish. ¹⁷ So Mordecai went away and did all that Esther had commanded him.

The call for such a time as this will take courage. It will take knowing your God. It will take knowing about the people whom you are called to go in front of; it will require understanding protocol. It will also take favor. At the same time, it requires that you grow not weary in well doing, you shall reap if you faint not. Part of the process is that you do not get weary while you are in training and preparation for such a time as this. What if Haddassah (Esther's Jewish name) had given up, or if as Esther she said she couldn't do it? The favor may have been years ago, months ago, or days ago, but that favor was not just for you, but for the future and those you are connected to. Favor to save an entire nation (generation) from annihilation; this favor also brought provision because the plan of the enemy was now turned around to not be a curse, but a blessing which caused unexpected increase.

Another aspect is that when Haddassah's name was changed to Esther, Mordecai told her to keep the fact that she was a Jew secret. The King did not know that she was a Jewess. We have to be careful with sharing our story. Some stuff you just don't tell. It is not that you don't be transparent, but some things you will have to keep silent about, pending God's timing. When striving to be in the will of God, only talk about the things the Holy Spirit tells you to talk about in that season. In the text she was told to conceal the matter; then later told to reveal it. We can look at Mordecai here as the Holy Spirit who leads and guides us and will tell you when it is time to bring up a subject or when it is time to walk away from it because He knows the timing. The Holy Spirit is part of the "for such a time as this" and He can speak through whomever He pleases, but it will always be a word of confirmation and edification that brings peace. Notice that she did not fly off the handle about this task. She prayed about it, she fasted about it, and sought the Lord. So for those called for such a time as this, you can not just run off at the mouth and tell everything. Then you also must be a person of prayer and supplication.

> (Romans 8:28) We are assured and know that [God being a partner in their labor] all things work together and are [fitting into a plan] for good to and for those who love God and are called according to [His] design and purpose.

If we truly trust that God is the Sovereign Ruler who is in control of all things, we will be sensitive to Him and the leading of the Holy spirit.

> (Ecclesiastes 3:1) TO EVERYTHING there is a season, and a time for every matter or purpose under heaven.

All of the topics discussed in this book prior to this point have been a set up for such a time as this in your individual life, as well those that you are *assigned* to impact for the kingdom. Understanding our faith is rooted in Jesus and the authority that we have as kingdom citizens in the earth realm, will empower us for the "such a time as this" *assignments*. In chapter 2 we discussed different points of preparation that every Christian faces, all set ups for the "such a time as this" *assignments*. Looking at how it is important to show up for what God has called us to do, and looking at the matters of the heart are all set ups for the "such a time as this" *assignments*. Recognizing that we are not of this world, and that we will still have to deal with temptation are all set ups for the "such a time as this" *assignments*. Seeing distractions as detours, yet continuing on for the purposes of God are all set ups for the "such a time as this" *assignments*. Getting a better understanding of the call to pray and war, just another set up for the "such a time as this" *assignments*. And God continually reconciling the hearts of His people and us getting in line with our part are all set ups for the "such a time as this" *assignments*. Look at our greatest example in Jesus, He prepared His entire life for the one week ministry of Calvary. Our *assignments* do not end in physical death, but there will be some things that die off in the process, and God brings resurrection power on the scene.

CHAPTER 11 – KINGDOM READY

11.1 Kingdom ready

Like in *A Portion Volume One*, the entire purpose of this book has been leading up to being kingdom ready, and bringing as many people with you into the kingdom of God.

Evangelism – all have a part to play in evangelizing the earth realm for the kingdom. Give the gospel presentation, coupled with the word of your testimony. You don't have to have a pulpit or a license to share what God has done and how He has changed your life since you began to know Him more intimately. We have come to think of evangelism as something only evangelist do; or ministers; or pastors – but this is not true. All believers have a part to play in it. My pastor taught a series titled "Evang-ology" where he defined evangelism as being twofold: winning the lost; and growing the found. I refer to this second *portion* as cleaning the fish – which involves assisting believers in the transforming of their minds according to the word of God. Helping people truly understand salvation (redemption) and what it entails as well the sanctification process. God is also concerned about this because His desire is that all men be saved and come into the knowledge of Him (see 1 Timothy 2:4). This growing knowledge is helping us be prepared for eternity in God's kingdom.

11.2 Eternity Minded

Do you want to be remembered in eternity for the decisions you make today? This will help us live as obedient servants, when we keep in mind that we are not living for the right now only, but for eternity. When we keep eternity in mind, it helps us in our weary moments and helps us make better decisions. Knowing that eternity will remember the decision I make now – will help me make kingdom minded decisions in the present – and will assist me with on all the various *assignments* this journey will take me on.

> (Ecclesiastes 3:11) He has made everything beautiful in its time. **He also has planted eternity in men's hearts and minds** [a divinely implanted sense of a purpose working through the ages which nothing under the sun but God alone can satisfy], yet so that men cannot find out what God has done from the beginning to the end.

Our spirit man is created in the image of God (Genesis 1:26-28), and God's spirit is eternal. This is why as a 3-part being, spirit/ body/ soul, we must be born again in the spirit realm through faith in the Lord Jesus Christ which gives us heavenly entry into eternity – not hell bound. Because you will spend eternity with God (absent from the body is present with Christ, 2 Corinthians 5:8) whether in hell or heaven, because He made them both; the decision as to which you will spend eternity in is based on your soulish decision to receive or reject the Lord Jesus Christ as Savior. Human beings will spend about 80 – 110 years in the earth realm, and FOREVER in eternity – all based on the soulish decision to accept or reject the 3rd person of the godhead, Jesus, as Savior. Being eternity minded will cause you to reprioritize your entire life:

> (Matthew 6:33) But seek (aim at and strive after) first of all His kingdom and His

righteousness (His way of doing and being right), and then all these things taken together will be given you besides.

I know this text in context is talking about what you will eat and wear, but it is also talking about worry. Seeking the kingdom, God's way of doing things, will reduce worry in this earth realm and alleviate a lot of the excuses we make for not doing the 2 great things we are commanded to do.

11.3   The Great Commandment and The Great Commission

> (Matthew 22:36-40) Teacher, which kind of commandment is great and important (the principal kind) in the Law? [Some commandments are light—which are heavy?] [37] And He replied to him, You shall love the Lord your God with all your heart and with all your soul and with all your mind (intellect). **[38] This is the great (most important, principal) and first commandment.** [39] And a second is like it: You shall love your neighbor as [you do] yourself. [40] These two commandments sum up and upon them depend all the Law and the Prophets.

> (Matthew 29:18-20) Jesus approached and, breaking the silence, said to them, All authority (all power of rule) in heaven and on

earth has been given to Me. **¹⁹ Go then and make disciples of all the nations**, baptizing them into the name of the Father and of the Son and of the Holy Spirit, ²⁰ Teaching them to observe everything that I have commanded you, and behold, I am with you all the days (perpetually, uniformly, and on every occasion), to the [very] close and consummation of the age. Amen (so let it be).

The great commission and the great commandment have been discussed in principle throughout this book. To quote Rick Warren "A great commitment to the Great Commandment and the Great Commission will make you a great Christian." So truly the only way to be great is to be committed to love and fulfilling the commission to make disciples for the Lord Jesus Christ.

I have listed the text for the great commission and commandment here, this is what we are to be obedient in doing: loving and making disciples. The love of God gives us access to the kingdom through salvation in the Lord Jesus Christ – a free gift for all who will accept it. Then, because we have received this love, and are growing in our understanding of it in our life, and for all mankind, we will do our part in making disciples and as Matthew 29:20 implies, not just catching fish, but cleaning them by teaching to observe what Jesus has commanded, getting God's people ready for eternity by setting our minds on kingdom.

> (Matthew 4:19) And He said to them, Come after Me [as disciples—letting Me be your Guide], follow Me, and I will make you fishers of men!

11.4 Conclusion

Take a moment and look over the table of contents now – notice how all of these topics tie into being a better disciple and being an epistle of love. In the introduction, obedience is a life long journey, and being obedient to the great commandment of love will make it easier to be a part of the great commission. Chapter one, when our faith is firmly rooted and grounded in the Lord Jesus Christ, when we truly understand our authority in Him and the help of the Triune God, we are better equipped to be eternity minded and help get disciples in the kingdom. The largest chapter, chapter two discussed several topics of being on *assignment*, and if you notice, they all point toward discipleship and love – becoming a better disciple personally. Chapter three shows us the importance of accepting our *assignments* and walking in them – all in preparation for the kingdom – for us, as well as for others. Getting our hearts right in chapter four is an important step in the process of being kingdom ready, eternity minded, and in line with the great commission and commandment.

Recognizing that we are not of this world in chapter five is a definite preparation for kingdom disciples to get rooted in. And understanding that temptation is always present, but learning how to deal with it when we fall to it, and continue hot for God in chapter 6 – again, having our minds set on eternity will help us over it all. I am reviewing the titles of the chapters to conclude the book and show you that it is all about being kingdom ready, eternity minded, walking and being a part of the great commission and the great commandment. So be on the lookout for distractions, as discussed in chapter seven, that can either be from God or the enemy. Chapter eight addresses the role of prayer and fasting while on *assignment* – which is required equipment in the kingdom ready process. Chapter nine, reconciling the hearts, is showing God's desire, and why we must be making our way through each of these topics discussed in this book, culminating in this last chapter. Each and every one of us holding this book has a call for such a time as this, as discussed in chapter ten. My desires are that you have been expanded in your personal understanding of your *assignment* and some of the tests and obstacles that will appear.

In concluding this chapter and this project, I would like to encourage you to continue in the *assignments* that God has placed before you as the *obedient* servant you are designed to be. Know that you are not alone, God has several of His children going through the preparation of a life time.

<<<NOTES>>>

Thank you for your generous support of "A Portion Ministries" – You may contact us for further information, to request speaking engagements, and to share love gifts at the following:

Email: paulettex7@gmail.com

Facebook: Paulette Denise

www.ingramcontent.com/pod-product-compliance
Lightning Source LLC
Chambersburg PA
CBHW031251290426
44109CB00012B/529